ALIVE
in
the **Spirit**

Books by A.W. Tozer

ALIVE

in

the Spirit

EXPERIENCING THE
PRESENCE AND POWER OF GOD

A.W. TOZER

COMPILED AND EDITED BY JAMES L. SNYDER

BETHANYHOUSE

a division of Baker Publishing Group
Minneapolis, Minnesota

© 2016 by James L. Snyder

Published by Bethany House Publishers
11400 Hampshire Avenue South
Bloomington, Minnesota 55438
www.bethanyhouse.com

Bethany House Publishers is a division of
Baker Publishing Group, Grand Rapids, Michigan

Printed in the United States of America

Library of Congress Control Number: 2016942353

ISBN 978-0-7642-1807-1

Unless otherwise noted, Scripture quotations are from the King James Version of the Bible.

Scripture quotations marked ASV are from the American Standard Version of the Bible.

Cover design by Rob Williams, InsideOutCreativeArts

James L. Snyder is represented by The Steve Laube Agency.

16 17 18 19 20 21 22   7 6 5 4 3 2 1

Contents

Introduction

The subject of this book, *Alive in the Spirit*, is a very crucial theme for the day in which we live. No other subject could be as controversial as dealing with the Holy Spirit.

One of the things that impressed me as I collected A.W. Tozer's sermons in preparation for this book is that Tozer says the evangelical church of his day treated the Holy Spirit as the liberal modernistic church did the person of Jesus Christ.

The liberals did not deny Jesus; they more or less ignored him. And the evangelicals in Tozer's day did not deny the Holy Spirit; they more or less ignored Him and His rightful position in the church. His observations are still true today.

Tozer implies that the evangelical church is going down the same path that the liberal churches did. That being said, he offers a possible solution to bring our churches back under the authority of the Holy Spirit.

The authority of the Holy Spirit must begin with the individual Christian and then flow over into the local congregation.

Our strategies are backward. Local church leaders and even denominational leaders are trying to set the tone for the congregations to follow. They have boiled it down to a despicable term (from Tozer's perspective)—a *formula*. All you need is the right formula and everything will be all right.

The focus in this book is on the individual. Yes, there are some encouragements for local assemblies, but the emphasis is on the individual Christian. The local church comprises individual Christians, and as those individual Christians go, so goes the local church.

This was Tozer's passion and it is shown here in this book. He bemoans the fact that the evangelical church has been so divided that it has lost its influence in the culture. Instead of the church influencing the culture, culture is not only influencing the church, it is taking over the church. Tozer declares that what we find in the world we also find in the local church. This ought not to be so.

Tozer's presentation does not go to extremes. The problem is that one group goes to a far extreme and another group goes to the opposite far extreme—the exhibitionists on one end and the cessationists on the other. This has done critical damage in the church, as Tozer notes. The only way to remedy this is to put the doctrine of the Holy Spirit in its proper perspective. That is what this book does.

In one chapter, he talks about his love of great paintings and says that a painting is not comprised of just one brushstroke, but of many. When you look at that painting you are not conscious of one brushstroke. When you become conscious of one brushstroke, you lose the picture altogether. This, Tozer says, is what has happened concerning the doctrine of the Holy Spirit.

To understand the Holy Spirit and His rightful place of authority in the life of the believer, and then in the life of the congregation, we have to surrender personal opinions and prejudices. It is critical to check everything with the Word of God.

Tozer often proposes that people can take a verse of Scripture out of context and make it say anything they want it to say. But each verse must be read in the context of the entire Bible. It takes all the Bible to make the whole Bible. When we splinter the text, pulling out a single brushstroke, we lose what it is all about.

His view on the gifts of the Spirit is that they are not to promote any one person. When one person or even one gift is exalted in a congregation, it is probably not the work of the Holy Spirit. This sounds harsh, but we need to get serious about the work of the Holy Spirit in our lives and in the life and ministry of the local congregation.

Tozer is very careful not to attack individuals or even denominations, but he does attack errors of doctrine. As a man of God called to do the work of God, he felt an obligation to speak out against the spiritual errors of his day. The thing that is most amazing to me is that the sermons forming the basis of this book were preached in the late 1950s and early 1960s. I have to remind myself that Dr. Tozer died in 1963. What he said then is true today and even more so. The warnings he gave then apply to our situation today.

I believe that if a person takes this book seriously, it will deeply affect their spiritual life. The end goal is to become *Alive in the Spirit.*

According to Tozer, one of the things that has replaced the work of the Holy Spirit in the local church is entertainment.

Our society is obsessed with entertainment, and this has come into the church of Jesus Christ. Tozer objects to this. Worship and entertainment are opposites and cannot be mixed. It is either one or the other.

The problem Tozer had with entertainment is that it always promotes a person. Even though that person may mention Jesus or God and claim to be a Christian, the focus is really not on God but on the person and the performance.

I chuckled when I heard Tozer tell the story of a person who wrote to him explaining that singing a hymn was a form of entertainment. He said, "If that's entertainment, then I'm an entertainer." But he quickly followed by saying, "It's not and I'm not."

He went on to explain that his top priority in life was to be a worshiper. It was the purpose and focus of the Holy Spirit in his life to exalt Jesus Christ and to bring into his life the spirit of worship. The same should be true of us today. Worship is critical, and for Tozer, worship could not be man-induced. Worship that does not start with the Holy Spirit is not true worship.

Tozer suggests that our worship services today are man-centered and man-promoted as a result of neglecting the authority of the Holy Spirit in our congregations. As such, they cannot exalt Jesus Christ.

Throughout this book, he says that people can do good works, but they are not the kind of works that promote and accomplish the holy work of God. Only the Holy Spirit can do the holy work of God. It begins with the Holy Spirit and it ends with the Holy Spirit.

This book reflects the passion Tozer had for the body of Christ.

Throughout the book, I've tried to capture Tozer's tone, which is conversational. In some sermons, I discovered him sharing his testimony, and I thought that was very good to include here. He is not talking about something that he heard about or read about, but rather something he experienced personally. His testimony both of being born again and being filled with the Holy Spirit lays the foundation for what Tozer says throughout this book. I found the influence of the Holy Spirit in his life and his daily walk fascinating.

This book is not to be read in one sitting. Although it could be, you will not reap the greatest benefit by doing so. Reading a chapter at a time and then pausing and thinking about it and applying its truths to your heart is really what Tozer intended. This is not simply literature to be enjoyed, but spiritual truth to be absorbed on a personal level. Knowing *about* the Holy Spirit is different from *knowing* the Holy Spirit by personal acquaintance. That is Tozer's emphasis throughout.

Dr. James L. Snyder

1

My Experience
With the Holy Spirit

Therefore if any man be in Christ, he is a new creature: old things are passed away; behold, all things are
become new.

—2 Corinthians 5:17

No subject could be more crucial to the church today than the Holy Spirit. I know nothing that inspires me more than meditating on the Scriptures concerning this third person of the Trinity.

I hope to cover the subject as thoroughly as possible, although I realize the limitations I have. No matter how much I know about God, there is much more I do not know. My daily passion has been to pursue God and to know Him as fully as He desires to be known.

In dealing with the subject of the Holy Spirit, I know I will interject my opinions. This is something that cannot be helped. If I do not have an opinion about the Holy Spirit, why am I talking and writing about Him?

My opinions, however, must be based on truth as revealed in the Scriptures by the Holy Spirit. The apostle Paul encouraged his readers not to trust what he had to say because he was saying it, but rather to search the Scriptures to make sure he was telling the truth: "These were more noble than those in Thessalonica, in that they received the word with all readiness of mind, and searched the scriptures daily, whether those things were so" (Acts 17:11). And so, at the beginning, I want to encourage you not to trust or believe what I have to say without collaborating everything with the Word of God.

Later on I will devote a chapter to the foundation of my belief in the Holy Spirit. That is, the Scriptures, the creeds, and the hymns. These three sources together form a harmony of truth about the Holy Spirit, and my opinions need to be in line with them. If there is anything I believe about the Holy Spirit not substantiated in this trio, I need to have the intellectual and spiritual integrity to cast it aside.

Everyone has the right to give testimony of their life in the Spirit. That testimony has to be collaborated, as I have pointed out, with established truth going all the way back to apostolic days. I want to give my testimony. Sometimes I am a little awkward in sharing personal things about my spiritual life, but I think it necessary for you to understand that what I am talking about in this book is something I have experienced personally. I am not just talking theory but truth I have personally experienced.

There are several ways to deal with the doctrine of the Holy Spirit. The first way would be to study what the Bible has to say about the Holy Spirit, and then to read all the books written on the Holy Spirit. This is the theological aspect. I want you to understand I believe in theology. Theology is simply the study of God, and I treasure nothing more in my life than the study of God. Sometimes, our study of God is merely technical and not personal. But if it is biblical truth, it has personal application to everyday living. We must do more than just believe the truth; we must allow the truth to transform us radically into new creatures in Christ.

Certainly I want to talk about the technical aspects of the Holy Spirit and what the Bible teaches as well as the doctrine associated with this blessed third person of the Trinity. However, that is just the beginning. I have built my personal experience upon that foundation, and the Holy Spirit has been an important aspect of my life from the very beginning.

My Conversion

I was not born into a Christian family. My parents were fine people from western Pennsylvania, but they were not Christians. When I was a teenager, our family moved to Akron, Ohio, where the rubber factories were employing many people, and my sister and I got jobs there.

Just down the street from where we lived was a Methodist church. Occasionally we would visit, but not regularly. I went more than the rest of my family because I met a young lady there who later became my wife. The primary attraction at that Methodist church, I must admit, was this young lady.

I still was not a Christian, even though I listened to the sermons of the preacher. Basically all he said was that if you want to feel good, just do good, and everything will be okay. Well, that has never really resonated in my heart and soul, even today.

Looking back, I thank God for the winsome ways of the Holy Spirit in dealing with the heart of such an untaught lad as I when I was only seventeen. We had a neighbor by the name of Holman. I do not remember his first name; we just called him Mr. Holman. He lived next door and we were told he was a Christian, but he never talked to me about Christ.

One day, as I was walking up the street with this friendly neighbor, he suddenly put his hand on my shoulder and said, "I've been wondering about you—if you're a Christian, if you're converted. I just wanted a chance to talk it over with you."

I told him I was not a Christian, and that seemed to be the end of the conversation. Perhaps the Holy Spirit planted a seed in my heart at this time.

Three years after moving to Akron, I was walking home from work when I noticed a small crowd of people on the opposite side of the street. They were gathered around an old man who seemed to be talking. At a distance I could not hear what he was saying, and so out of curiosity I walked across the street to see if I could hear what all the commotion was about.

The man had a strong German accent, and so it was hard for me to understand him. I really didn't know what was going on. But then it dawned on me: This man was preaching right out on the street corner. I was a little amazed by this. And shocked, to be truthful. I thought, *Why doesn't this man go to church and preach? And it isn't even Sunday!*

However, curiosity got the best of me, and I tried to listen and understand what he was saying. Then he said something that seemed very clear to me: "If you don't know how to be saved, just call on God, saying, 'God, be merciful to me a sinner,' and God will hear you."

I heard nothing else because that phrase pierced my heart and I could not get away from it. I walked home and carefully thought about what the man had said. I had never before heard words like those. I had gone to church a few times, but never heard the gospel in such a straightforward manner.

I must confess it awakened within me a gnawing hunger to find out if what this man was saying was true. There began within me a hunger for God that has persisted until this day.

All I can say, looking back, is that the Holy Spirit was at work in my life. I did not know the Holy Spirit at the time, and I did not know how He worked, but my ignorance of the situation did not in any way limit the Holy Spirit from working in my life.

When I got home, I went straight up to the attic, shut the door, got on my knees, and poured out my heart to God. Even to this day, I am not sure what really happened at that moment. All I can say is this: I was born again. The Holy Spirit birthed in my heart a new life I had never before experienced.

This encounter with the Holy Spirit transformed my life and started me on a path of pursuing God. I was just seventeen.

Being Filled With the Holy Spirit

I began dating the young lady I had met at the Methodist church. Her name was Ada Cecilia Pfaust. Eventually we would get married, but our relationship brought me in touch with Ada's mother, Kate Pfaust, a deeply spiritual person and part of a Pentecostal church in the Akron area. I had no idea what a Pentecostal church was all about. To me, church was church.

She would invite me to prayer meetings at her home and have me speak, and she encouraged me in the area of ministry. I had no training, but I had plenty of help and guidance from her. I can see now that the Holy Spirit was behind this encounter.

One day Kate took me aside and had a very serious talk with me. It was concerning being filled with the Holy Spirit. The Methodist church I was going to never mentioned this at all. In fact, the Holy Spirit was rarely referred to.

I did not quite understand what she meant by being filled with the Holy Spirit. Who is this Holy Spirit? But she encouraged me and prayed with me, and then one day she said, "Young man, you must get down on your knees and die to yourself before the Holy Spirit will fill you." And she explained in great detail what this meant, as much as I could understand.

I know the Holy Spirit was working in my life because there developed within me a restlessness. I was at the place where I wanted everything God had for me, even though I did not quite understand it all. I did not understand the Holy Spirit. I did not understand what being filled with the Holy Spirit was all about. But I was open to everything God had for me, and I was not going to let my ignorance limit God's work in me.

Then it happened. I was nineteen years old when I was baptized with a mighty infusion of the Holy Spirit. Even now, it is hard to explain what happened. I have had years to think about it, study it, and meditate on it, and yet when the Holy Spirit does something in you, it is usually beyond your ability to totally comprehend it, let alone explain it.

I know what God did for me and within me at that time. Nothing on the outside from then on had equal importance for me. In faith, I took a leap away from everything that was unimportant to that which was most important, which was to be possessed by the Spirit of the living God.

Looking back over my life, my testimony is simply that any work God has ever done through me and my ministry dates back to that moment when I was filled with the Holy Spirit. All the credit goes to the Holy Spirit. That is when I truly became alive.

Everything I endeavored to do on my own was a failure. Whenever I got out of the way and allowed the Holy Spirit to work, He did a marvelous work. The work of the Holy Spirit in the life of a person surrendered to Him has eternal value.

It's All About the Spirit

If anyone is going to be blessed by God and used by Him, it will begin with a mighty infilling of the Holy Spirit in their life. From that point on, they are no longer in control, but the Holy Spirit is working in and through them. This is why I am so enthusiastic about the Holy Spirit, being filled with the Holy Spirit, and the work of the Spirit, which I will explain more thoroughly in this book.

I think one of the great challenges of my life has been to step aside and allow the Holy Spirit to do His work His way. Pride sometimes gets in the way, and I begin to think that I am doing a great job. The Holy Spirit usually lets me know it is not my doing anything, because anything I do fails most miserably. I am not in the business of promoting myself; I am in the business of surrendering to the Holy Spirit and allowing Him to do a work that only He can do.

Throughout the years, I have learned not to dictate to the Holy Spirit and try to point Him in the direction I think He should go. I must confess I do not understand all that the Holy Spirit does. Much is behind the sacred curtain of His divinity, which no man dare step through.

What the future holds for me only God the Holy Spirit knows. I do not even want to try to guess. Sure, there are things I would like to accomplish, and I believe every man is immortal until his work is done. In addition, I believe that the Holy Spirit can use me as long as I am willing to be used by the Holy Spirit. My goal is to live in the Spirit each day.

The most important thing I have learned in my experience with the Holy Spirit is to make sure it is indeed the Holy Spirit working and not me. When I have become too confident, I have made some bad mistakes. It is important for me to get alone with the Holy Spirit on a regular basis and allow Him to do His work in my life. What the Holy Spirit does *through* me is dependent upon what the Holy Spirit can do *in* me.

Not a day goes by but that I give myself completely to the Holy Spirit. I want to be very careful I am not doing something in my own strength. I will explain the difference between doing something in my own strength and something in the power of the Holy Spirit in a later chapter.

Since my conversion—which resulted in my being filled with the Holy Spirit—to this very moment, my life has all been a work of the Holy Spirit.

Nothing is more crucial to my daily pursuit of God than my commitment and surrender to the person of the Holy Spirit.

Blessed Holy Spirit, I honor Thee and bless Thee for Thy patient work in my life. Amen.

REFLECTIONS

Think about your conversion experience and what happened that day.

Can you identify with being filled with the Holy Spirit?

What has been the influence of the Holy Spirit in your life?

My Perception
of the Holy Spirit

Howbeit when he, the Spirit of truth, is come, he will guide you into all truth: for he shall not speak of himself; but whatsoever he shall hear, that shall he speak: and he will show you things to come.

—John 16:13

To expand on my testimony concerning life in the Spirit, I want to outline what the Holy Spirit really means to me and how He has influenced my life. I know the danger of focusing too much on the Holy Spirit, and I know those who focus exclusively on Him are in danger of abusing the truth.

However, in this book, I want to focus on the Holy Spirit.

The Holy Spirit and My Ministry

My journey began, of course, with my conversion and was accented by my being filled with the Holy Spirit. That, however, was only the beginning. From that moment on, I have been walking in fellowship with God. Not a perfect walk, I assure you. Those who claim to have a perfect walk probably do not understand the Scriptures in this regard.

The fact that my walk is not perfect has encouraged me to always fall back on the Holy Spirit and His guidance and strength. Sure, I have tried to do things in my own strength. My enthusiasm for doing the things of God sometimes gets the best of me. I think the Holy Spirit understands that and allows me to fall flat on my face so that I realize what His position in my life is all about.

The Holy Spirit has opened several avenues of ministry, from preaching on street corners to preaching in churches to preaching in Bible conferences. He has also opened ministries for me on the radio as well as a great ministry in the area of writing. I did not start out to be a writer, but the Holy Spirit motivated me in such a way that writing became a vehicle through which He could work through me.

I humbly give testimony to the fact that my book *The Pursuit of God* has been used in ways I never would have imagined. I hear from people whose lives have been deeply challenged and changed through reading that book. I am amazed at the effect it is having.

Did I write that book? Well, I worked at the typewriter, but it was the Holy Spirit working through me who wrote it. The praise and honor go to Him alone.

Ministry is like that. Whenever God can get an instrument willing to be used as dictated by the Holy Spirit, He will use that person for His glory, not theirs. I have seen God work in ways I could never have imagined.

If I were planning my life, I would not be where I am today. My ministry has been a step-by-step walk with the Holy Spirit. Many times He opened a door I did not know was there. Opportunities have come my way I never could have planned myself. Then, to be perfectly honest, He has shut a few doors. At the time, I did not understand why. Looking back, I can see why and thank God for it.

And so I want to give credit to the Holy Spirit for how He has worked in my life and developed in me and through me a ministry that I hope has blessed people, but more than that, has brought glory to God our Father.

As I look back over my life, I have to ask myself, *How did God use someone as uneducated as me?* I never finished the eighth grade. I never went to Bible college or seminary. I was the least educated person God could select to use for His honor and glory. This brings me to the point that God does not choose us for who we are, or how qualified we are, but rather for who He is and what He is permitted to do through our lives.

I cannot look back and say I accomplished a lot because of my education or my experience or anything else. I succeeded in nothing on my own. As I seek God every day, I believe He can do things through me that will bring glory to Him. Only when I get to the other side and see Jesus face-to-face will I really understand all He was able to do through my life. The things I look at now and appreciate will mean nothing when I see Him face-to-face.

So again, I give testimony that the Holy Spirit has deeply affected my ministry.

The Holy Spirit and My Worship

I also want to say that the Holy Spirit has deeply affected my worship. There is nothing I enjoy more than worshiping God, and I must confess my worship is not some contrived traditional ritual. I enjoy worship in the congregation of God's people gathered to sing the great hymns of the church and raise their voices in praise.

More than that, I enjoy getting alone and on my face before God and in silence waiting upon Him. As someone once said, "Prayer is wonderful and sometimes it employs words."

In the beginning, I had a long grocery list of things I wanted God to do. God has been very patient with me. As the years have gone by, that grocery list has shrunk to the point that I no longer bring a list before God. Oh yes, there are things I want God to do, but more than that, I want God to minister to me personally and then work through me.

I believe spiritual ministry flows out of a heart that has been in the presence of God. When we come into His presence, we begin to take on a ministry that can come from nowhere else. I have learned much about God on my face before Him in silence, and it has taken a while for me to adjust to that posture.

I have discovered much in my prayer life and in reading books on worship. When I come before Him, however, I need to put away everything, quiet my heart in silence, and allow the Holy Spirit to create the focus at that moment and let His presence fill me with wonder and awe.

Through the years, I have learned a bit about worship. I confess I have not learned everything yet, but when I come to worship God, I do not want to bring anything except a surrendered heart and mind.

One great asset in my worship is the hymns of the church. Unashamedly, I love the hymns. Daily I love to take out my hymnbook and sing one of the old hymns, comfortably off-key, but in deep praise and worship of God.

Those old hymn writers knew God in a way many people today could never imagine. In singing their hymns, I enter into the spirit of their worship and begin to acknowledge the priority of God not only in their world but also in my life.

I think this is the difference between those grand old hymns of the church and some of the songs being written today. I do not care *when* the song was written, I only want to know it focuses on God and how it can help me come into His presence. If that song is a hundred years old or a week old, it doesn't make any difference to me.

My Appreciation of the Mystics

Another medium the Holy Spirit has used in my life has been the old mystics of the church, the masters of the inner life. I know I can get into trouble when I use the word *mystic*, but I can handle it. I am not easily rattled. Looking at some of their writings, one thing grabs my attention: They knew God.

Many things about these people I probably would not agree with. But they knew about God. I want to know what they knew about Him, how they came to know it, and how that can impact my life. I don't care who the messenger is. If he brings me into the presence of God, I welcome him with open arms.

I could mention some of those by name, but there is no need. The Holy Spirit has brought into my life books, authors, and hymns that have been used to help me understand who God is and how God can be a priority in my life. That certainly is my goal, to be alive in the Spirit.

The Holy Spirit and My Attitude

The Holy Spirit has also affected my attitude. No one could be more grouchy or negative than I am. I can see a cloud in every silver lining, and I can be as critical and sarcastic as anybody you would ever know. I have relatives to prove that I could be just like them. I have inherited from my family an acid tongue.

Through the years, though, the Holy Spirit has worked on my attitude. I do not have to defend myself anymore. I do not have to make sure everyone understands what I am saying. I do not have to be right every time. My relationship with God does not rely on anything external. It is "Christ in me," (see Colossians 1:27) that truly matters.

For me to get to that point it had to be the work of the Holy Spirit. I cannot muster myself up, fill my head with positive thoughts, and go forward. I can honestly confess that I have been positively negative most of my life. If it were not for the Holy Spirit, I would be grouchy, cranky, and bitter at this point in my life.

But the Holy Spirit has made significant changes in my attitude. Although the Holy Spirit has come a long way with me, He probably has a lot further to go. Until my dying day, I want to surrender each day to the Holy Spirit to do that work in me that He wants to do. I will never dictate to the

Holy Spirit or demand that He do this or that for me. Every day of my life, I want to surrender myself to Him and allow Him to set the agenda of my day.

The Faithfulness of the Holy Spirit

This has not been easy for me. The work of the Holy Spirit in my life has cost me plenty. Looking back over my life, I rejoice in all God has done for me. I am a little sad at how I have made things hard for the Holy Spirit. But I really am no challenge for Him. Nobody is a challenge for the Holy Spirit. I am no worse or better than anyone else. The Holy Spirit does not have to work harder on me or softer on me than someone else.

The thing that has made the difference in my life has been getting to know the Holy Spirit on a personal level. This has been an ongoing factor in my life. I want to get away as much as I can and spend time alone with the Holy Spirit and fellowship with Him and allow Him to breathe into me the life and energy He wants me to have. I want every day to be a fresh experience with the Holy Spirit.

Each day of my life is a demonstration of the faithfulness of the Holy Spirit to work in a life that is trying to be surrendered to Him. It is not my imperfections that challenge the Holy Spirit, because He is perfect and works according to His perfections.

I try to be honest and forthright in my talking about the Holy Spirit. I want no one to think I am just pontificating on the doctrine of the Holy Spirit. I want everyone to understand that this Holy Spirit has made a difference in my life. When I talk about the Holy Spirit, I am talking about

Someone whom I know personally and intimately. It is not just doctrine, although doctrine is good and wonderful. I have gone beyond doctrine into the fellowship of the Holy Spirit and have personal experience to back it up.

Doctrine explains *who* the Holy Spirit is. The next step is to fellowship with and experience the Holy Spirit in ways that cannot be explained in human terms.

I have said it often: If you can understand it and explain it, it is probably not the Holy Spirit working. He woos me unto himself. He invites me into His presence. He desires for me to know as much about Him as I am capable of processing at the time. And what a wonderful life it has been.

Holy Spirit, how grateful I am for Thy tireless work in my life. Amen.

REFLECTIONS

Think about how the Holy Spirit has influenced your life.

Where have you surrendered to the Holy Spirit in practical ways?

How has your relationship with the Holy Spirit redefined you?

3

My Warning to the Church

Yet if thou warn the wicked, and he turn not from his wickedness, nor from his wicked way, he shall die in his iniquity; but thou hast delivered thy soul.

—Ezekiel 3:19

Before going further with this important subject, I need to put forth a personal word of warning. I want to set forth the condition of the church today as I see it and then suggest a recommendation I believe will set us going in the right direction.

God's Work Depends on His People

Whenever God moves, He always starts with His people. This has been His course of action throughout the Scriptures

31

and church history. God's people are connected with God in such a way that He is able to do what He desires to do. The prophet of old said, "If my people . . . shall humble themselves . . ." (2 Chronicles 7:14). The focus of everything God does is His people.

This puts the responsibility on God's people. We have desires, ambitions, and programs, and we try to push them forward not knowing that God has a well-laid-out plan for us. Reading about revivals, beginning in the Old Testament to the present time, every revival brought people back to the place where they left God. This is where God always begins.

Our insistence on going forward without God's blessing, or as I shall point out in this book, His anointing, means that we do it without the approval of God and therefore without the power of God. God's self-imposed limitation and restriction is His people, which is the foundation on which God delights to work. Whenever God gets ahold of someone who is totally surrendered and one He can trust, God begins His work. The quality of the work is not so much in the individual as it is in the individual possessed by God.

God has chosen to work within the confines of His redeemed people. This being true, it is imperative that God's people get in line with God and His will as revealed in His Word by the Holy Spirit.

A Warning

I want to begin with a dire warning.

To say the evangelical church of today has a great challenge before it is only to state the obvious to the discerning heart. What I hope to do is define that challenge and outline the direction in overcoming this difficulty before the church. Too many in the church are oblivious to this challenge. A great awakening needs to take place among evangelicals once again to bring the church back to that place of divine blessing that once marked her.

For the evangelical church to go forward in the power and demonstration of the Holy Spirit, it needs to deal with all the baggage accumulated over the years. Many love their baggage, and it will prove difficult for some to rid themselves of it. Each generation believes they have the right perspective on spiritual things and are convinced they know better than their forefathers. This has never been the case, and all you have to do is read church history to understand this.

To go forward requires that we go backward to rediscover and reclaim our spiritual roots. We have abandoned our roots and are wandering helplessly in a spiritual desert, which in my opinion is the problem today.

David understood this when he posed the question "If the foundations be destroyed, what can the righteous do?" (Psalm 11:3). Indeed, what can the righteous do? My attempt in this book is to answer that question and to do so from the biblical perspective. It does not matter what we believe—if we cannot prove it and verify it in the Scriptures it is not worth believing.

The question "What can the righteous do?" needs to be asked today. First, we need to understand what the foundations of the righteous are. What has been destroyed or is in danger of being destroyed in the evangelical church today? Unless we know this and deal with it, we are facing some very dire times, which, unfortunately, I believe have already begun.

A Prophecy

May I be allowed to prophesy? I know a man gets into deep trouble when he attempts this sort of thing. However, based on my study of the Scriptures, reading of church history, and praying over the subject for many years while watching the trends go up and down, I have come to a certain conclusion, which is the basis of my prophecy. This results from a burning passion within me for God and my love for the church of Jesus Christ.

Whatever anybody can say of me, they must admit that with everything within me, I love the church of Jesus Christ. I desire to do everything within my power to identify with the church and to help that church go forward in a way that will honor Jesus Christ. It pains me deeply to see the evangelical church in such a state, knowing the remedy is only a prayer away.

The next generation or two of Christians will face a challenge that cannot be overcome in the natural. Throughout history, God has selected certain people to come out of the established church and start over again using biblical authority.

What is happening across the board cannot be salvaged from a spiritual standpoint, and the chances are pretty high that God may have to start all over again. My prayer is that it happens quickly.

Read church history; read about the revivals and how God scrapped everything present at the time and started all over again. Perhaps this will happen again. I pray it will.

Unless there is a real surrender to the Holy Spirit, we are facing some serious problems. We have become a culture of Christians trying to do God's work apart from the enduement of the Holy Spirit in our lives. We acknowledge Him in our creeds but rarely in our work and in our lives.

Leanness in Our Souls

Just as in the Old Testament and the nation of Israel, many today believe they are what God wants. They believe, like Israel of old, that nothing bad can happen to them. And so they will continue to go forward as they always have.

One of the most alarming passages in the Old Testament seems appropriate for today. David wrote concerning Israel, "They soon forgot his works; they waited not for his counsel: But lusted exceedingly in the wilderness, and tempted God in the desert. And he gave them their request; but sent leanness into their soul" (Psalm 106:13–15).

Just because you have what you want does not mean what you have is what God wants you to have. I think the alarming phrase is *sent leanness into their soul*. Could that describe many evangelical churches across our country today? We have everything we want but there is that leanness in our soul that we cannot, or won't, deal with.

For the most part, many Christians are satisfied with the status quo and believe that what they have is what God has given them. It is this spirit of satisfaction that is the undoing of the evangelical church of our day. Our forefathers were never spiritually satisfied. They had a hunger for God that was all but insatiable. Their thirst for God drove them forward. They had a divinely inspired discontent that only God could satisfy.

The Problem With Being Content

We are being taught from evangelical pulpits today to be content. Whole series of sermons and multiple books focus on the subject of being content and happy where you are. As long as you are saved, you are on your way to heaven, so just relax and enjoy the journey, they say.

Our forefathers did not teach this.

An old saint once mentioned that he feared we have made the church to be for *us* instead of for Christ. We can only come into the true church through the door that is Jesus Christ, and once inside that church, everything is for God. The transformation that takes place at our conversion prepares us to come into the presence of God. God is not so much interested in coming into our world as He is in bringing us into His.

I understand it may be too much to ask Christians today to read history, read about the church in the day of its glory and the men and women who led the church in a path to victory and honor. Nevertheless, it is imperative that we read and understand our past. If we do not understand our past, we will never fully comprehend our future. What God has done in the past is what He will do for us today. "Jesus Christ the same yesterday, and today, and forever" (Hebrews 13:8). If I do not know what He has done, how can I have faith for what He will do for me today?

We need to know from where we have come, we need to know our heritage, and we need to know the message that has come down to us from the days of the apostles. That message has not changed.

I believe the job of a prophet is to rattle the spiritual cage and wake up sleepy Christians, calling them out to understand the danger that we face today. We have come to the point of contentment. We are content with where we are, we are content with what we have, and we have no real expectation of what the future holds. Henceforth, this generation of Christians and the next faces a grave and severe danger.

The Holy Spirit's Work Is Not About Numbers

Leanness of heart is seen everywhere. People are satisfied with what they have, and many preachers are satisfied with numbers. Our whole focus has become on how many people we have coming to our churches and how big the offering is. We have come to the point of worshiping numbers.

The Old Testament is filled with stories of how God worked contrary to numbers. Gideon's three hundred men is an example of this (Judges 7:7–8). God does not work within the confines of our strength; God works according to His character and nature and power. If we only see God work within our structure, we will never see God work at all.

If we would do the work of John Wesley, Martin Luther, David Livingstone, and A. B. Simpson, we need to know *how* to do it. We do not do the work of these men by imitating what they did. Certainly we are living in different times, and the work that these men and others like them did was a work for their time. We do not imitate the work they did, but rather we need the Holy Spirit that motivated and led them to motivate and lead us.

I cannot start a Reformation like Martin Luther did. However, I can have within me the same Spirit that drove him in that direction. It is the Holy Spirit that we need in our midst today.

We have come to worship numbers, methods, and programs all to no avail. We may have large numbers, but where is the Holy Spirit in our midst? Where is the power of His anointing on our services today?

We have a generation of imitators, but they are imitating external things. We need a generation of imitators of the Holy Spirit. The way to do that is not through outward imitation but through an inward surrender to the Holy Spirit.

Get all the education you can afford to get. But when it comes right down to it, it is not your education that will accomplish anything for the cause of Christ. It will be the Holy Spirit working in you and through you. Whatever it takes for the Holy Spirit to use me unconditionally is what I am willing to do.

My challenge for this generation is to stop playing religious games and take this matter of being the church of Jesus Christ as serious as our forefathers did. Do not settle for anything less than an influx of the breath of God from on high, a mighty enduement of the Holy Spirit in our lives, driving us forward in His power, accomplishing His goals.

James reminds us in the New Testament that God is not about numbers. "The effectual fervent prayer," James writes, "of a righteous man availeth much" (James 5:16). All we need is God on our side and we will be victorious. It must be noted that God will never compromise His character or nature for anyone or any situation.

We Must Hunger for God

If we are to be the church God can bless and use in this generation, we need to be so saturated with the Holy Spirit that everything within us illuminates the Spirit of God to the world around us.

God will move again. I am confident of that. History declares this truth repeatedly. The problem is there are very few people prepared for a move of God in their lives. I believe God will ignore most of the evangelical churches standing today. They have what they want, they are satisfied with what they have, and there is no room in their program for the Holy Spirit to do His thing.

God will select a person here and a person there all over the world, but He will ignore those satisfied with what they have. I want to be among those dissatisfied with the status quo and having a hunger so deep for the things of God that nothing else can satisfy it.

I am not sure this can begin in today's church, and I am absolutely sure it cannot begin in most denominations. It has to be that person who hungers and thirsts after God, cares not for the things of this world, but is "Looking unto Jesus the author and finisher of our faith" (Hebrews 12:2).

Holy Spirit, count me among those who desire Thee more than anything or anyone else. Amen.

REFLECTIONS

How would you evaluate your current standing with God?

What are you willing to give up in order to follow God unashamedly?

Will you be counted in that number of those who desire God more than anything or anyone else?

My Awareness
of the Holy Spirit

If the foundations be destroyed, what can the
righteous do?

—Psalm 11:3

Indeed, today's church is facing a great challenge. To be
victorious over this challenge we need to reexamine our
foundation.

In order to know what we can do, we need to understand
what our foundation is and then we can build on it. If we
don't know our foundation we cannot build on it and that
guarantees ultimate failure.

I want to introduce, as if for the first time, this amazing
foundation: it is the third person of the Trinity, the blessed
Holy Spirit. Throughout this book I will use the titles *Holy*

Spirit, *Holy Ghost*, and *Spirit of God* and mean exactly and precisely the same person.

I will focus on how He relates to the other persons of the Trinity, how He is presented in the Scriptures, and how He has influenced my life up to this very day.

When we come to the Trinity, we need to understand that all the persons of the Trinity are equal in every way. The presentation to us in the Scriptures may differ, but no difference exists between the three persons of the Trinity. What one is, the other two are as well. Therefore, I want to be very clear that when I am talking about the Holy Spirit here, I am singling Him out in order to present His work.

Often the danger is in the area of neglecting the person of the Holy Spirit. In the evangelical church, we do not deny this third person of the Trinity. After all, He is in our creeds and we do believe He exists. You cannot be an evangelical Christian without believing in the Trinity.

Our True Foundation

It is not our beliefs I am calling into question here; rather, it is the place of the Holy Spirit in our churches, in our lives, and in our ministries. Where does He fit? Is He truly the foundation of our lives and ministries? Or have we sadly replaced Him with something so far inferior that there is absolutely no comparison?

Although we know about the Holy Spirit theologically, we know little about the Holy Spirit functionally. I have been very careful in setting forth the truth that we need to have an experience with the Holy Spirit—based upon our theology, of course—something personal in our everyday life.

As I have mentioned, it is one thing to believe *about* God and it is quite another to *believe God*. Henceforth, it is one thing to believe *about* the Holy Spirit and quite another to believe in the reality of the Holy Spirit in personal experience. And not only personal experience, but also the experience of the local church. Where does the Holy Spirit fit into the local assembly?

Is it possible that we have replaced Him unknowingly? Is it possible that we have put in place things in the church today that replace His position and authority?

In many cases, the church today looks like a social club, a place to gather, have fun and fellowship, do things together, and then go home and get back to life as it is in reality. If what we do on Sunday morning is completely contrary to our attitude and practice the rest of the week, perhaps what we are doing Sunday morning is hypocritical. How is it possible for us to be one way one day and completely the opposite the next day?

If the Holy Spirit is the foundation upon which I am building my life and ministry, then everything about me will begin to take on the characteristics of the Holy Spirit. Where, in today's church, do we find these holy characteristics so dominant in the person of the Holy Spirit?

The World in the Church

I am disturbed by the evangelical churches' pulling aspects of the world into the church that are absolutely contrary to the Holy Spirit. Whatever is the latest trend out in the world soon finds its way into the church. I wonder how our Lord, who suffered on the cross for us, thinks about the levity that has come into our churches?

We are looking to the world to authenticate what we do. I may sound critical here, but if it looks like the world, it does not fit in the church and has no place. There is no way the church can accept into its fellowship the attitudes and agenda of the world and still be called the church of Jesus Christ.

I know there is pressure to win people and fill our churches today. We look to the world to see how they are filling up stadiums, concert halls, and theaters, and we are trying to adapt their methods to accomplish our goals. Friends, the two do not mix.

Then, when we get these people in the church by using the world's methods, we need to continue using the world's methods to keep them. The church with the latest method is the church with the largest crowd. We have trained this generation of Christians to follow the method instead of following Christ. People do not come to church anymore because Jesus Christ is glorified; they come to church because that is where they can be entertained and feel good about themselves.

Today's generation has become addicted to entertainment, and this spiritual virus has seeped into the church. If the only way we can get people is if we entertain them, the only way we can keep people is if we continue entertaining them with the newest and most popular form of entertainment.

We need to understand that the methods of the world cannot be used to accomplish the goals of God. We need to turn our back on the world completely and finally. We are not of the world and therefore we need to leave the world behind us and concentrate on the Lord Jesus Christ. The focus of the Holy Spirit will always be on Christ. Whatever is not focused on Christ is not the work of the Holy Spirit.

This is exactly what the Holy Spirit does. He cannot use the methods of the world, which are contrary to His holy nature and character. The Holy Spirit is God all the way through. And God will never compromise His nature or character for any reason or for anyone. The more I get to know the Holy Spirit, the more I will begin to understand what He does not want in my life and in the life of the local church.

Because the Holy Spirit is not dominating our assemblies as He once did, we are looking for ways to compensate. Rather, we should look for ways to submit ourselves completely to the Holy Spirit and allow Him to move in our midst in ways that will please Him. I believe some churches are so completely out of the hands of God that if the Holy Ghost withdrew, they would not find it out for three months.

Let me be clear here. I do not believe the Spirit of God ever leaves the church completely, but He can, like the Savior in the back of the ship, go to sleep and not make himself known, allowing us to get along without Him for years. How tragic and yet how true of today's churches. Our evangelical leaders are trying to fill a void only the Holy Spirit can fill.

What Is the Holy Spirit?

So much can be said about the Holy Spirit, but I think the most important question is "What is the Holy Spirit?"

He is a person. Jesus said, "But the Comforter, which is the Holy Ghost, whom the Father will send in my name, he shall teach you all things, and bring all things to your remembrance, whatsoever I have said unto you" (John 14:26).

Because the Holy Spirit is a person, He possesses all the attributes of personhood. He can feel. He can love. He can hate. He can be grieved. All the things attributed to personality can be found in the Holy Spirit. We need to understand He is a person and can be addressed as any real person.

When I begin to understand the personality of the Holy Spirit, I begin to develop fellowship with Him that would be impossible otherwise. If I do not know Him as a person, how can I have an intimate relationship with Him? It is really that simple.

People will acknowledge Him as a person, but then not go the next step and experience the intimacy of the Holy Spirit as a person. There has to be an intimacy, an experience between two personalities. Namely, the personality of the Holy Spirit and my personality or your personality must come together in fellowship.

The most important thing in the world is that the blessed Holy Spirit is now among us and in us. Jesus, in His body, is at the right hand of God the Father Almighty interceding for us, and He will be there until He comes again. In the meantime, He said, "And I will pray the Father, and he shall give you another Comforter, that he may abide with you for ever" (John 14:16). This Holy Ghost is Christ's representative, and He will be everything Jesus is and was and will be.

The Holy Spirit has a personality, individuality, intelligence, love, and memory. The Holy Spirit can communicate with you, He can love you, and He can be grieved and quenched when you ignore Him.

I am afraid that because we do not know Him experientially, we have grieved the Holy Spirit. Because the Holy Spirit can love, He can also be grieved. And I believe that is the status of the evangelical church today. We have grieved the Holy Spirit because we do not know Him as a person.

Yes, we know Him as a doctrine. Many can quote Scriptures and explain them to us. It is one thing to know *about* the Holy Spirit. It is quite another thing altogether to know the Holy Spirit in *personal* acquaintance. That is what is lacking today. We need to have such an acquaintance with the Holy Spirit that He becomes our best friend as we travel this pilgrim road.

Bring the Spirit Back Into the Church

I believe we need to bring the Holy Spirit of God back into the church, back by prayer, obedience, and confession, until He literally takes over. Then there will be life and light and power and victory and joy and fruit in our lives. We can live on a different level altogether, a level we never before dreamed possible.

Every church has an obligation to regularly examine itself to see if what it is doing is on the solid foundation of the Holy Spirit. The tendency is to drift, as the Scriptures often warn us. I need to be careful that my life is solid on that foundation. If I am not building my life and ministry on the foundation of the Holy Spirit, I will not be pleasing and glorifying to God.

When the Holy Spirit came on the day of Pentecost, His primary goal was to exalt Jesus Christ. I will talk more about this in detail in another chapter. But the evidence of the Holy Spirit in a person's life is the glorification of Jesus Christ. The evidence of the Holy Spirit in the local assembly is the glorification of Jesus Christ. When Christ is not glorified, the Holy Spirit is grieved and withdraws His influence from that person or that assembly. If the world is comfortable in the church it is only because Christ is not being glorified, which means the work of the Holy Spirit is being hindered.

Our goal is to keep on that foundation of the Holy Spirit and live out the life He directs.

Holy Spirit, I confess my moments of ignoring you. Forgive me. I want you to be the focus of my life. Amen.

REFLECTIONS

How has the foundation of the Holy Spirit affected your day-to-day living?

What are some ways in which you can make sure you are building on that foundation?

Focus on the evidence of the Holy Spirit in your life.

5

The Threefold Foundation for Trusting the Holy Spirit

And if one prevail against him, two shall withstand him; and a threefold cord is not quickly broken.

—Ecclesiastes 4:12

We have at our disposal a marvelous threefold cord, enabling us to understand the Holy Spirit as God intended Him to be understood. To comprehend the Holy Spirit, we need to get a perspective of what the historical church said about the Holy Spirit. Since the day of Pentecost, God has not changed His mind.

I would like to focus in this chapter on this threefold cord: the Scriptures, the creeds of the church, and the hymns of the church. These three guard the church against heresy. All three agree concerning the doctrine of the Holy Spirit. Nothing has changed to in any way invalidate what the church has believed from the very beginning.

The Scriptures

The first cord would be the Scriptures. This is where we must always begin. What is not built upon the Scriptures will not stand and is not of God. If we have anything in the creeds or hymns not in full alignment and harmony with the Scriptures, we need to repudiate it. But all three form a threefold cord that cannot be broken.

> Whither shall I go from thy spirit? Or whither shall I flee from thy presence?
>
> Psalms 139:7

That is omnipresence, and not even the devil is omnipresent. Only God can claim this quality, and this psalm attributes omnipresence to the Holy Spirit.

> By his spirit he hath garnished the heavens; his hand hath formed the crooked serpent.
>
> Job 26:13

Here the breath, the ghost, the spirit of the Almighty, who has given the Holy Spirit, is said to be a Creator. He issues commands: "And the Spirit of the Lord fell upon me, and said unto me, Speak" (Ezekiel 11:5), and only God can do that.

> The grace of the Lord Jesus Christ, and the love of God, and the communion of the Holy Ghost, be with you all. Amen.
>
> 2 Corinthians 13:14

> Now the Lord is that Spirit: and where the Spirit of the Lord
> is, there is liberty.
>
> 2 Corinthians 3:17

This is but a sampling of Scriptures about the Holy Spirit and His place in the Trinity. It would do you a world of good to search the Scriptures to see what they say and teach about the third person of the Trinity. No study could be more beneficial to your everyday life.

The Church Creeds

Today, many Christians are so busy reading Christian fiction they never get around to reading the creeds written by the church fathers. My advice is to periodically take the time to go through these creeds. Allow me to give a sampling of them as they relate to the Holy Spirit.

What do the creeds say about the Holy Spirit? To know this is to know what the early church believed the Holy Spirit to be. And He has not changed. These creeds are a declaration by the church fathers of what the Scriptures taught.

The Nicene Creed (AD 392)

> We believe in the Holy Spirit, the Lord, the giver
>   of life,
> who proceeds from the Father [and the Son],
> who with the Father and the Son is worshiped and
>   glorified,
> who has spoken through the prophets.

The Athanasian Creed (c. AD 415)

Whoever wants to be saved should above all cling to the catholic faith. Whoever does not guard it whole and inviolable will doubtless perish eternally.

Now this is the catholic faith: We worship one God in trinity and the Trinity in unity, neither confusing the persons nor dividing the divine being. For the Father is one person, the Son is another, and the Spirit is still another. But the deity of the Father, Son, and Holy Spirit is one, equal in glory, coeternal in majesty. What the Father is, the Son is, and so is the Holy Spirit. Uncreated is the Father; uncreated is the Son; uncreated is the Spirit. The Father is infinite; the Son is infinite; the Holy Spirit is infinite.

Eternal is the Father; eternal is the Son; eternal is the Spirit: And yet there are not three eternal beings, but one who is eternal; as there are not three uncreated and unlimited beings, but one who is uncreated and unlimited. Almighty is the Father; almighty is the Son; almighty is the Spirit: And yet there are not three almighty beings, but one who is almighty. Thus the Father is God; the Son is God; the Holy Spirit is God: And yet there are not three gods, but one God. Thus the Father is Lord; the Son is Lord; the Holy Spirit is Lord: And yet there are not three lords, but one Lord.

As Christian truth compels us to acknowledge each distinct person [in the Trinity] as God and Lord, so the catholic [universal] religion forbids us to say there are three gods or lords.

The Father was neither made nor created nor begotten; the Son was neither made nor created, but was alone begotten of the Father; the Spirit was neither made nor created, but is proceeding from the Father and the Son. Thus there is one Father, not three fathers; one Son, not three sons; one

Holy Spirit, not three spirits. And in this Trinity, no one is before or after, greater or less than the other; but all three persons are in themselves, coeternal and coequal; and so we must worship the Trinity in unity and the one God in three persons.

The Apostles' Creed (AD 390)

I believe in the Holy Ghost, the holy catholic Church, the communion of saints, the forgiveness of sins, the resurrection of the body, and the life everlasting. Amen.

I am not sure what reading these does for you, but it is like a chicken dinner to my soul. This declaration of faith has come down through the years, and this is what our Fathers believed. When that company of Christians met and declared these truths, some of them had their tongues pulled out, their ears burned off, their arms torn off, and some lost a leg, all because they stood for this: that Jesus is Lord to the glory of God the Father. These men were martyrs who had not quite died, but were maimed horribly. They were the old saints of God and learned scholars who knew the truth. They wrote these creeds and gave them to us and to the world for the ages. I thank God on my knees for them.

The Hymns

The hymns of the church form our third cord. I hardly know where to start or stop. I can mention only a few of my favorites. Check these out in your hymnal:

- "Spirit of God, Descend Upon My Heart" by George Croly (1780–1860)

- "Breathe on Me, Breath of God" by Edwin Hatch (1835–1889)
- "Come, Holy Spirit, Heavenly Dove" by Isaac Watts (1674–1748)
- "Holy Ghost, With Light Divine" by Andrew Reed (1787–1862)
- "Gracious Spirit, Holy Ghost" by Christopher Wordsworth (1807–1885)
- "Holy Spirit, Faithful Guide" by Marcus M. Wells (1815–1895)
- "Come, Sevenfold Holy Spirit" by Albert B. Simpson (1843–1919)

O COMFORTER, GENTLE AND TENDER

O Comforter, gentle and tender,
O holy and heavenly Dove;
We're yielding our hearts in surrender,
We're waiting Thy fullness to prove.

Refrain
We're waiting, we're waiting
For Thee, O heavenly Dove;
We're yielding our hearts to surrender,
We're waiting Thy fullness to prove.

Come strong as the wind o'er the ocean,
Or soft as the breathing of morn,
Subduing our spirit's commotion
And cheering when hearts are forlorn.

Refrain

O come as the heart searching fire,
O come as the sin cleansing flood;
Consume us with holy desire,
And fill with the fullness of God.

Refrain

Anoint us with gladness and healing;
Baptize us with pow'r from on high;
O come with Thy filling and sealing,
While low at Thy footstool we lie.

Refrain

Albert B. Simpson

Where do we stop? Meditating on these hymns enables us to understand what the church has believed down through the centuries. I know many churches are not singing hymns anymore, and for the life of me, I cannot understand why. Those hymns connect us with the church of the past. Many people want to cut themselves off from the past, spiritually speaking. It is impossible. The hymns are part of that threefold cord.

The Holy Spirit Is God

The Holy Spirit is an important aspect of the Christian church today. We baptize in the name of the Father, Son, and Holy Spirit.

If the Spirit was not God, but something less—if He were a man or an angel or something else—if He was not God, as some say, then I have a question for you. If the Scriptures do not teach that He is God, how would it sound if we baptized in the name of the archangel Gabriel? Or suppose I said, "I baptize you in the name of the Father and of the Son and of St. Paul"?

If I said, "I baptize you in the name of the Father and of the Son and of the Virgin Mary," that would be a horrible thing. You cannot attribute deity to St. Paul; you cannot attribute deity to the virgin, although we honor her for she was the mother of our Lord (the mother of our Lord's body, not the mother of our Lord's deity, for His deity had been before the foundation of the world).

Suppose we introduce Gabriel the archangel, and say, "The grace of our Lord Jesus Christ, the love of God and the communion of the archangel Gabriel"?

Everyone would shout, "Heresy, heresy, heresy!" And they would be right. It would be a terrible thing to introduce an archangel, an angel, or a human being where the Holy Spirit belongs. The Holy Spirit is God, and the most important fact is that the Holy Spirit is present among us today. An unseen deity is present.

We cannot hide from the Holy Spirit, for He is present in our midst. He is among us and He knows what is happening. He is indivisible from the Father and the Son. He is God, exercises all the rights of God, and merits all our worship, love, and obedience.

The Holy Spirit Is the Spirit of Jesus

That is who the Holy Spirit is, and here is the beautiful thing about the Holy Spirit: Being the Spirit of Jesus, you will find Him exactly like Jesus. People claiming to be filled with the Spirit but acting every way except like the Spirit have frightened some. Some say they are filled with the Spirit and are very stern, harsh, and abusive; others do weird things, claiming that it is the Holy Spirit. But the Holy Spirit is exactly like Jesus, just as Jesus is exactly like the Father. Jesus said, "He that hath seen me hath seen the Father" (John 14:9), and, "But the Comforter, which is the Holy Ghost, whom the Father will send in my name, he shall teach you all things, and bring all things to your remembrance, whatsoever I have said unto you" (John 14:26). The Holy Spirit will demonstrate Jesus Christ to us.

For example, what does the Holy Spirit think about babies? Well, what did Jesus think of babies? Jesus thought of babies just as the Father did. And the Father must think wondrously well of babies because Jesus asked that babies be brought to Him that He might bless them (see Matthew 19:14–15). Theologians may not know why He did it, but I think I do. Nothing is sweeter and softer in the world than the top of a baby's head, and Jesus put His hand on that little head and blessed that baby in the name of His Father.

What does the Spirit think of sick people? What did Jesus think of sick people? What does the Spirit think of sinful people? What did Jesus think of the woman dragged into His presence, accused of adultery? The Spirit feels exactly the same way Jesus feels about everything. He is the Spirit of Jesus and acts exactly the way Jesus acts.

The Holy Spirit is friendly. Some try to make Him out to be something else than friendly. Because He is friendly, He may be grieved by our ignoring Him, resisting Him, doubting Him, sinning against Him, refusing to obey Him, or turning our backs on Him. We can grieve the Spirit, and He can be grieved because He loves. If you do not love, you cannot grieve.

When the Scripture says, "And grieve not the holy Spirit of God, whereby ye are sealed unto the day of redemption" (Ephesians 4:30), it is telling us that He loves us so much that when we insult Him, He is grieved. When we ignore Him, He is grieved. When we resist Him, He is grieved. When we doubt Him, He is grieved.

But we also can please Him by obeying and believing. When we please Him, He responds just like a pleased father or mother responds.

A Call for Restoration

The restoration of the Holy Spirit to His rightful place in our life and the life of the true church is by all means the most important thing that could possibly take place. Unless the Holy Spirit is feelingly and consciously in our midst, you might as well be somewhere else.

It is entirely possible to run a church without the Holy Spirit. A church can be organized, elect a board, call a pastor, adopt a constitution, and that is all there is to it. The Holy Ghost can leave the pastor turning the crank and nobody finds it out for five years. Oh, what a horrible tragedy for the church of Christ that we do not recognize this. "He that hath an ear, let him hear what the Spirit saith unto the churches" (Revelation 2:7).

One of two things will happen in response to this: a disinterested reaction to it or an eager seeking for Him. I am praying for the latter. I believe we need to have eager seeking for better things than we have now. The question is "Are we going to seek God together? Are we going to stand by that threefold cord and be a testimony to our generation?"

We stand firm on the Scriptures, the creeds, and the hymns. "A threefold cord is not quickly broken" (Ecclesiastes 4:12).

SPIRIT OF GOD, DESCEND UPON MY HEART

Spirit of God, descend upon my heart;
Wean it from earth, through all its pulses move;
Stoop to my weakness, mighty as Thou art,
And make me love Thee as I ought to love.
George Croly, 1780–1860

Blessed Holy Spirit, I accept Thee and all the majesty of Thy divine revelations. Amen.

REFLECTIONS

Spend time meditating on the creeds.

How would you define your personal trust in the Holy Spirit?

Give the Holy Spirit opportunity to fill your life anew.

6

The Penetrating Voice
of the Holy Spirit

And the Lord came, and stood, and called as at other
times, Samuel, Samuel. Then Samuel answered, Speak;
for thy servant heareth.

—1 Samuel 3:10

A Lost World

We are living in a lost world. By that I mean the inhabitants of
the world are lost, not dramatically or poetically, but really and
individually. Much of religious verse makes a very beautiful
picture of a lost world—and the world is never to blame, they
are just unfortunately lost. But there is nothing poetic about
being lost, as there is nothing poetic about having cancer. The
human race is lost only because individuals composing the
human race are lost with a mighty calamitous visitation of woe,
which all the eloquence of human speech could never describe.

The worst part about our lostness is that it is inside of us. I am speaking of people born in the world who know trouble with the world and its lostness. A man lost in the forest knows he is lost and may find his way out. However, a man lost in the forest with amnesia who cannot remember his name or where he belongs is lost with a lostness that is not only external but also internal.

Human beings are lost with an internal lostness making them insensible to the fact that they are lost. Or at least they scarcely know they are lost.

This is not a question we need to take to the theologians and inquire, "Dr. So-and-So, are people lost?" Either the doctor repeats the Scripture back to you or the doctor is not a trustworthy man. It is not debatable. It is not something old-fashioned and believed only by a few. It is a fact as real as gravity or mathematics or any other fact. The fact is the world is lost. But it is also a fact that though lost, it is not forsaken.

Through the atoning blood of the Lord Jesus Christ, God has made an everlasting covenant, a compensation for our sins. He has atoned and made it right, and Christ is the propitiation for our sins, which means the world is not forsaken. It is lost, its lostness is deep inside, and mostly it does not know how lost it is. God knew it was lost and found the way to make full reparation and pay the full price so that mankind can now be redeemed.

LOVE FOUND A WAY

Love found a way, to redeem my soul,
Love found a way that could make me whole.

Love sent my Lord to the cross of shame,
Love found a way, O praise His holy Name!
                                    Avis M. Christiansen

God Is Speaking

God is speaking by many voices. He is speaking, for instance, by the voices of conscience, love, reason, death, and the Holy Spirit. Of all the clear, loud, distinguishing voices, the voice of the Spirit is the clearest and loudest. The voice of the Spirit gives grave and serious meaning to any other voice. Not all the theologians in the world could argue with someone lost or show that there was a way back unless the Holy Spirit was present to make that person see that truth in their own heart. It is possible to see a thing without understanding and never know what is in our hearts at all.

Two kinds of knowledge are available to you: the knowledge you have in your mind and the knowledge you have experienced. The Holy Ghost has a wonderful and mysterious way of making you experience the knowledge you only previously held in your mind. So God can say, "Adam . . . Where art thou?" (Genesis 3:9), and "Ho, every one that thirsteth" (Isaiah 55:1), and "Come unto me, all ye that labour and are heavy laden" (Matthew 11:28). The Holy Spirit gives meaning to these calls and to these voices.

The Confirmation of the Holy Spirit

Our Lord said when He, the Holy Ghost, comes, He would not leave you comfortless, but would come to you (John 14:18). But what was He to do? When the Comforter came,

He would confirm three things. He would confirm the words of Jesus, the works of Jesus, and the person of Jesus. When a man called Jesus of Galilee walked on the earth, He spoke the loftiest words ever spoken by any religious leader since the beginning of time, and He made the most astonishing, astounding claims for himself.

I am reasonably familiar with the writings of the great religious teachers of the non-Christian religions, and I can say that nobody ever made the claims for himself that Jesus made. No other religious teacher said, "Before Abraham was, I am" (John 8:58). Nobody else said, "I beheld Satan as lightning fall from heaven" (Luke 10:18). Nor did any say, "I and my Father are one" (John 10:30). No other teacher promised, "I go and prepare a place for you" (John 14:3). No other teacher said, "Destroy this temple, and in three days I will raise it up" (John 2:19). No teacher dared say, "I am the way, the truth, and the life: no man cometh unto the Father, but by me" (John 14:6).

These are astonishing claims, lofty words. The Holy Spirit came as a silent, penetrating, immediate witness to give confirmation to Christ's words.

The words of Christ cannot be confirmed by theological knowledge. Rather, it is the penetrating, wonderful words and presence of the Holy Ghost that give power to the Word.

Then there are the works of Jesus.

Nobody could deny that Jesus performed miracles, and even His enemies did not try. There is no way they could deny what was right before them. The only thing they could do was deny that God performed them. "This is the work of the devil," they said. Yet there was no denying the miracles. Jesus raised the dead, made the lake calm down in a storm, gave sight to the blind, and turned water into wine at a wedding. He did all these things, and the Holy Ghost confirms the divine quality of these works and proves they were truly of God.

The Holy Spirit also confirms the person of Jesus Christ.

Who else is like this man? Who else ever lived in the world like this man called Jesus?

Jesus was raised from the dead. The Holy Ghost has come in His confirmatory work. The mysterious Witness is now with us. Christ is no longer on trial as He was when He walked among men. Now man is on trial.

This whole matter of the religious question has been transferred from the schoolroom to the heart. There is a throne, and a man sits on the throne. The man is Jesus Christ the Lord. There is a throne where no one can come who might want to dethrone Jesus Christ the Lord. The Man sitting on that throne is invested with authority, power, judgment, and justice, so He can wield all authority in heaven and on earth. The man is Jesus Christ the Lord, and the Holy Ghost is here to witness to Him within our hearts. When Jesus spoke, He spoke in the ears of the people, but the Holy Ghost penetrates the heart and speaks in a way that even Jesus could not speak while on the earth.

The Conviction of the Holy Spirit

Jesus said that it was better if He went away, because He would send the Comforter, and when He came, He would convince the world of sin, righteousness, and the judgment to come. "Nevertheless I tell you the truth; It is expedient for you that I go away: for if I go not away, the Comforter will not come unto you; but if I depart, I will send him unto you" (John 16:7).

This holy Witness is present and in all things speaks for Christ. As you treat the voice of the Spirit, you treat Christ. The fate of every one of us depends not upon the historical evidence but upon the Holy Spirit. If you had to take historical evidence and figure out whether Jesus was the Son of God or not, the scholars and those who know how to take evidence and draw conclusions might make up their minds that Jesus was the Son of God, but the simplehearted and the unlearned of the world cannot do that. They would not know the laws of evidence and could not possibly arrive at a proper conclusion concerning Jesus Christ, even though the facts were given. The Holy Ghost leaps past all reasoning and all collecting of evidence and all taking of testimony to the conscience, taking this matter of Jesus and our relationship to Him out of the realm of reason altogether. Our faith does not rest upon nor depend upon historical evidence, but upon the invisible presence witnessing to the inner life and our response to that voice.

That inner voice will make use of historical facts, but does not depend upon reason working on those historical facts. When someone stands in the power of the Holy Spirit to preach the gospel, the Holy Ghost is with that person and confirms the Word with signs, which may be external or in the heart and conscience of the listener. It is the heart and conscience I am particularly interested in. While the preacher speaks, the Holy Ghost waits and watches and decides and selects, always selecting people out from the world.

Nobody can deceive the Holy Ghost. The preacher can be deceived, but the Holy Ghost is never taken in. He is never deceived because He is God, that invisible presence, the most important One in our midst today.

The Holy Spirit is like a pungent fragrance in the room. Like an X-ray, He goes clear through and through.

The Holy Spirit penetrates our minds and hearts about three vital truths:

> And when he is come, he will reprove the world of sin, and of righteousness, and of judgment: Of sin, because they believe not on me; of righteousness, because I go to my Father, and ye see me no more.
>
> John 16:8–10

"Sin, because they believe not on me"—that has led some to teach that unbelief is the only sin. No, unbelief is a sign, proof, and presence of sin.

This brings me to the point that faith is not an intellectual thing. It is a moral thing, a thing of conscience and of life and of living and of the Holy Ghost. Not a matter of reason at all. He said He would convict the world "of sin, because they believe not on me." He will show that their unbelief results from their sin.

A generation ago, they were saying it is no longer the sin question, it is the Son question. Everything depends on whether you believe Jesus is the Son of God or not. Sin does not matter. I never believed that and I believe it less now. The problem is not the Son question because that was taken care of when the Holy Ghost came. The problem is the sin question. "If any man will do his will, he shall know of the doctrine, whether it be of God, or whether I speak of myself" (John 7:17). Anybody who believes in Jesus Christ and who wants to do the will of Christ will know this, and the Son question is settled.

The Holy Ghost settled the question of whether Jesus was the Son of God when He came down at Pentecost. Therefore, it is the sin question that matters now.

You believe that Jesus is the Son of God, and when the Holy Ghost has pierced your heart with your own sin, you will believe it. You will not believe it because you read five books to prove it; you will believe it because that is the Holy Ghost's business to witness to the person and works and words of Jesus and confirm that He is the Messiah, the Son of God.

Unconfessed sin makes saving faith impossible. People struggle to believe mainly because they are hanging on to their sin. A person who loves their own sin does not believe. You cannot believe if you have sin in your heart.

The Comforter also came to pierce, convince, and convict about righteousness, because Jesus said, "I go to the Father" (John 16:10).

Conspicuous proof of the world's moral condition is that one righteous man alone stood in the world and they would not have Him. Jesus Christ was the one supremely holy man, and they said, "We will not have this man to reign over us" (Luke 19:14).

As the Spirit persists, one of two things will happen. He will persist until you surrender to His voice, say yes, and believe on His Son actively, or until the voice can no longer be heard. When the voice can no longer be heard, you will think the voice is no longer speaking. But it is the death of the heart. When the heart dies and the troubling voice of the Spirit can no longer be heard, then sinners imagine things are all right: They have heard wrong and think things are not as bad as they expected or thought. They let their hearts die, their conscience no longer can be pricked, and they cannot feel anything because the Holy Ghost's penetrating, piercing words are no longer a bother to them. They imagine all is right now and there comes a relief, even pleasure sometimes. For after the heart the Spirit has worked on for a long time has resisted, deceived, and lied to God, the voice of the Spirit is heard no more.

Jesus sent the Holy Ghost, and when He is come, He will convict the world. He did not say the church, but the world. The unbelievers of the world are those He is talking about.

Those who can still feel the sting of the Holy Ghost ought to thank God on their knees, for many people's hearts are dead. They are not against religion, nor are they for it. They are simply dead. They died a long time ago. They are the walking dead, like those men on the ship in *The Rime of the Ancient Mariner* who stood up without souls in them, their bodies doing the work, pulling their ropes. Dead men standing on the deck.

Some have deadened their hearts by disobedience, others by lust, others by love of money, others by love of pleasure, others by holding grudges. They will not give up. Others by the unforgiving spirit, others by bitterness, others by a temper they cannot and will not control, others by persistent gossip, whispering behind backs, others by downright lying, others by dishonesty in their business, others by the filthiness of their personal conduct.

Little by little, the voice dies and ceases to be heard because the heart has grown deaf. "He that hath ears to hear, let him hear" (Matthew 11:15).

The plain implication here is that there are some who do not have ears to hear, but it seems that whoever has ears had better perk up and listen, for the Spirit is calling.

I have no doubt He is calling some who think they are saved and some who wish they were saved and some whose fellowship is broken and who are far from Christ.

"The Spirit and the bride say, Come" (Revelation 22:17), and He is come to convict the world of sin and righteousness and judgment and to call them on to Christ. That entreating voice still stands. If you can hear the voice, happy are you.

HUMBLE THYSELF TO WALK

Humble thyself and the Lord will draw near thee,
Humble thyself and His presence shall cheer thee;
He will not walk with the proud or the scornful,
Humble thyself to walk with God.

Johnson Oatman Jr.

Holy Spirit, let Thy voice penetrate my heart and lead me down the path of obedience to Thy Word. Amen.

REFLECTIONS

Try to remember the last time you felt conviction.

How did this change your prayer life . . . for yourself? for others?

The Dissimilarity the Holy Spirit Emphasizes

Even the Spirit of truth; whom the world cannot receive, because it seeth him not, neither knoweth him: but ye know him; for he dwelleth with you, and shall be in you.

—John 14:17

The Christian faith teaches a complete antithesis and contradiction between the world and the true church. The spirits here are sharply different from each other. There is a sharp difference between the spirit of fallen man and the spirit of redeemed man.

Primary Differences

Primarily, the difference is that they are incompatible with each other. They are not conformable to each other and are even hostile toward each other. Between the spirit of the world and the Spirit of Christ there can only be forever inconsolable enmity. It was that Spirit in Jesus that the world recognized; not the Roman world, but the religious world. They recognized that Spirit in Jesus as their natural enemy. So they rose up against Jesus and crucified Him because He had in Him a Spirit which, altogether apart from anything He said and did, brought hostility between them and Him. This is a very hard thing to tell people because it is not what we are hearing today. It is what the Bible teaches; it is what our church fathers and the Pilgrims and Puritans taught.

Now this antithesis, this flat and violent contradiction between two spirits, accounts for all the persecution that has ever taken place down through the ages. He who is born once always persecutes he who is born twice.

No Compromises

There can be no compromise between the two; there can be no reconciliation between them: the spirit born once and the spirit born twice, the man born of the flesh and the man born of the Spirit. This message has almost been lost from the church today. We do not attempt to make our faith acceptable to the wisdom of the world or to society in general. We admit no necessity to make our religion acceptable to them or to have what they now call "dialogue."

That is a lovely little expression. We have what are called political dialogues, and so now, not to be outdone, we have religious dialogues. Dialogue consists of two people talking, but talking does not sound learned enough, so now we call it dialogue.

Those of the world have a spirit and have been baptized in that spirit. That spirit is a fallen spirit and alienated from God; it is evil and blind. The god of this world blinds the minds of unbelievers and fills them with vanity, hypocrisy, stubbornness, lies, pride, and all the rest. Therefore, the world cannot receive the Spirit of Christ.

Whenever you hear anyone saying God is going to pour His Spirit out upon all humanity, you know they are wrong, because the Scripture says the world cannot receive the Spirit (John 14:17). He pours His Spirit out and makes Him *available* to all flesh, but even when the Holy Spirit was poured out at Pentecost it was only poured out on the one hundred twenty who were prepared. The rest did not receive Him because they were not prepared to receive Him. It takes a work of God in the heart to enable anyone to receive this new Spirit, which is of God.

Today we are not supposed to be sure of that. We are supposed to harmonize everything, get everybody together, and work out of the general religious situation a common pattern that will please everybody.

That is not the way God sees it, for the world cannot receive this Holy Spirit. They cannot understand the man who has been regenerated; they cannot understand repentance; they do not know what it means. They cannot understand faith; they have no concept of what faith means. They cannot understand the new birth, so they call it joining the church. They do not know what it is to be born of the Spirit and of water and washed in the blood. They do not know what redemption means. The world cannot understand Christ. "No man," Jesus said, "can come to me, except the Father which hath sent me draw him: and I will raise him up at the last day" (John 6:44).

The Importance of Illumination

There must be an illumination from heaven. When Peter said, "Lord, thou art the son of God," Jesus said, "Blessed art thou, Simon Bar-jona: for flesh and blood hath not revealed it unto thee, but my Father which is in heaven" (Matthew 16:17). Any religious truth passed on from one to the other passes from one mind to another mind, but there is an illumination from heaven that is completely different.

The Holy Spirit alone can enter and make the depth of our heart's sin real to us. Nobody can repent until he knows the depth of his own sin, and nobody can know the depth of his own sin unless the Holy Spirit shows it to him. No one can repent properly until the Holy Spirit shows him, and the person outside of Christ cannot understand this divine communion.

While the world knows nothing of the depth of its own sin, yet God has His elect. They are not morally better than other people by nature. God does not select people with a religious bent. Some people have a religious bent, some a poetic bent, some a musical bent, and some an artistic bent. Some people can take photographs and make them look very natural and beautiful without ever having a lesson in their life. Some people by nature are religious, but that is not what God is talking about. The religious bent is not what is meant here. The man God finds, saves, gives of His illumination, and of the Spirit is not necessarily morally better than any other.

Jacob was not morally better than Esau. David was not morally better than Saul.

Who are these that in the midst of a fallen world manage somehow to get through and are touched in a right sense? God lays His hands upon a man, God calls a man, speaks, and rouses him, and he is awakened. God enlightens him and moves upon him and it is this that makes a Christian. He hears a message declared in Sunday school, from the pulpit, reading a tract or the Bible, or in a testimony, but he hears God calling, and so that touch of God comes upon him. He hears that call: "My sheep hear my voice, and I know them, and they follow me: And I give unto them eternal life" (John 10:27–28).

If you are a Christian, you are a miracle and something odd to the world around you. This is a strange day when you cannot tell a Christian from a sinner. A half-saved Christian from a half-saved sinner. You cannot tell one from the other, and everybody runs together with little distinction.

Down through the centuries, armies had uniforms and wore those uniforms in battle. In war, the soldiers mostly knew each other by their uniform. In more recent times, what little traces of morality there may have been in war disappeared during the Second World War. For example, sometimes the uniform of the other side was worn to infiltrate and get past the enemy line. Instead of the lines being tight between British and Nazi soldiers, between American and Japanese soldiers, they intermingled with the other side. The enemy took our uniforms and many a man died because he walked up innocently to a man wearing a uniform with his own insignia on it. He thought it was his own and died because he had been trapped and betrayed by the other side.

Separation From the World

In times past, the church and the world were separated so they at least knew where they stood. The world did not like the church and tried to kill all Christians. Tertullian said, "The blood of the martyrs is the seed of the Church." He also emphasized that there is no use killing Christians because every time you kill one, three others spring up. So they quit trying to kill them and set about wooing them. When they stopped trying to kill them and began to woo them, they won.

Today the world is not trying to kill us as such. Rather, it is trying to make us harmless by pulling out our claws and teeth and turning us into harmless tabby cats purring by the fireside while the world marches to hell. The world passes by and says, "What pretty kittens they are." God means we should have the life of God in us as a spirit within us. The world should know that, and there should be a sharp division.

If you are having trouble where you are working, do not let it bother you at all. It is a good thing you are having trouble. Let no one say you are a fanatic or you are wrong. If you are living for Christ and people not living for Christ are making it hard for you, thank God every night when the workday is done that you were counted worthy to suffer for the Lord Jesus Christ. Remember, "Ye have not yet resisted unto blood, striving against sin" (Hebrews 12:4).

Our Lord is coming back, and when He does, He will come back for His sheep. There will be many sheep running around and even goats in sheep's clothing. The sheep know the Shepherd's voice. When they hear the sound of His voice, they will start, and the goats will say, "Where do they think they are going?" They are going up to meet the Shepherd because they recognize the Shepherd's voice. They listen to the voice down here and they will listen to the voice up there; the goat does not know the Shepherd's voice. I believe the Spirit of God knows what He is doing. Upon those who have had a change and an infusion of the Spirit, God makes His great bestowal.

I think it is a great mistake to think everybody in the world is a scoundrel. Maybe I have been guilty myself in that capacity, sometimes making out, unintentionally, that the dividing line between the world and the church, sinners and Christians, is the dividing line between all the good people on one side and the rapists and the dope fiends and the embezzlers and the liars and the cheaters and the murderers over on the side of the lost. We leave the impression that over on the side of the church there are nice people, and they are the converted people, but that is not necessarily so. There are many kinds of lost people; people who commit rape, embezzle, murder, rob banks, and shoot the guards are just one kind.

Then there are the gentlest, kindest, friendliest, most cultured lost people, and these would invite you into their homes and treat you beautifully. They remember you at Christmas and do nice things for you, but they are of the world. The Christian is one who has been changed by the bestowal of the gift of God: eternal life in the Spirit. He belongs to a different race altogether. He is a completely different person. The world cannot receive the new creation. Not even the good world, the educated world, or the cultured world can receive it. Kind people cannot even receive this because they have another spirit. It is the spirit of the first Adam, but not the Spirit of the last Adam, which is Christ.

The Dividing Line

There is a dividing line, and my longing, my dream, my hope is that we should be a company of the ransomed ones, a company who has the second Adam, the new Spirit, the Spirit of the Shepherd, and who knows the Shepherd's voice. This new Spirit of Christ comes to the souls of men.

The world out there listens to us talk and thinks what we talk about is ridiculous. Maybe they think it is meaningless, so they are bored with it. Maybe they think it is offensive, so they are insulted by it. Some do not make any response at all. They are the hard ones to deal with. If you try to be a soul winner, do not worry about the man who asks you every kind of question. The man who glares and tells you, "Don't worry about me." The man who looks with glassy eyes and has no reaction at all, nods and smiles, but does not know what you are talking about, he is the hard one.

Then there is this blessed Holy Spirit. Christian groups are those anointed with the Spirit of Christ, that new Spirit of the regenerate world. That Spirit will someday take over and fill the universe. The blessed Spirit of God in Christ.

God grant that we hold up holy living in humility, repentance, obedience, faithfulness, cross-carrying, and an assembly on whom the Spirit can rest as the dove rested and as the clouds and fire rested upon Israel.

COME, HOLY SPIRIT, HEAVENLY DOVE

Come, Holy Spirit, heavenly Dove,
With all Thy quickening powers;
Come, shed abroad the Savior's love,
And that shall kindle ours.

Isaac Watts

I thank Thee, blessed Holy Spirit, that Thou hast called me to leave the world and follow Thee. So I do, in Thy power and for Thy glory. Amen.

REFLECTIONS

Think of how different your life is from the world.

Would Jesus be comfortable following you in your every-day activities?

What would you miss if you sold out completely to Jesus?

The Vitality of the Holy Spirit in the Church

Then the spirit took me up, and I heard behind me a voice of a great rushing, saying, Blessed be the glory of the Lord from his place.

Ezekiel 3.12

The Holy Spirit makes a big difference in the Spirit-filled church, and the difference is overwhelming.

If you would compare the average church of today in America with the average church in the apostolic age, you would find a great difference. And the difference would not simply be exterior. Yes, I acknowledge the fact that many things have changed. But the outward things that have changed are not the important things.

The important things are the interior aspects of the Spirit-filled church, those things that pass on from one generation to the next and really make the church what God wants the church to be.

Authority

In the early apostolic church, there was authority. Not man's authority. It was not a group of people coming together and voting on something and then the vote became the authority. Their authority was the manifest presence of the Holy Spirit in their assemblies. They did not gather because they had nothing better to do.

One instruction Jesus gave the disciples before ascending into heaven was "Tarry ye in the city of Jerusalem, until ye be endued with power from on high" (Luke 24:49). There was a power coming upon them that would be the absolute authority in their worship and in their ministry.

I often wonder in worship services today: *Who is really in charge? Where is the authority behind some of the worship happening in our churches?* I question whether it is really the authority of the Holy Spirit as it was in the days of the apostles. We must get back to the source of real authority, which is the Holy Spirit.

A Spirit-filled church cannot operate apart from the authority of the Holy Spirit. What happened on the day of Pentecost was the impartation of God's authority on that local church. The Holy Spirit in the lives of individuals filled with the Spirit administrates that authority.

Passion

The early church was not governed by Christians who had influence out in the community and brought that influence into the congregation. No, it was the authority of the Holy Spirit working through men and women who were absolutely surrendered to the Holy Spirit.

This not only affected their worship as they gathered, it also influenced their passion to reach the world for Jesus Christ. They were not satisfied with simply coming together on Sunday and singing a few hymns, taking up an offering, listening to a pathetic sermon that had no real point, and then going back to the life they were living the rest of the week. These men and women were so impassioned and empowered by the Holy Spirit that their desire was to reach their world for Jesus Christ.

This kind of power is needed in our assemblies today. We need a passion dating back to that early church because their passion was stirred and birthed by the Holy Spirit.

Revival

I think what we need today is a good old-fashioned revival. I do not like to use the word *revival* because it has been abused in the house of its friends. Most revivals today are simply an enthusiastic meeting, perhaps with a guest speaker, that does not change anyone. In fact, it often leaves folks the same as when they came in.

If you study the old-time revivals, those meetings changed not only people's lives, but the community as well. There was a power that did not come *from* the assembly, but a power that came down *on* that assembly—and that power was the Holy Spirit.

Just as Jesus promised that the disciples would enter into a new era of power and authority and lead the church of Jesus Christ in that direction, so should we be doing today. The agenda of the early church needs to be our agenda. I think it wise for us to study the early church, the early leaders, and discover what motivated them, and what they were motivated to do.

What Did *Not* Happen at Pentecost?

Going back to those early days of the church, before the ascension of Christ, Jesus promised the disciples that a new power would come upon them, the power of the Comforter. The Holy Spirit would lead them in power and authority such as they had never before known.

To put this in perspective, I need to pose a serious question: What did *not* happen on the day of Pentecost? I think it is something we need to think about.

Prior to the day of Pentecost, the disciples enjoyed many blessings of God. Pentecost did not initiate this. They were already blessed.

Prior to Pentecost, the disciples were truly converted and had wonderful fellowship with Christ. In fact, I think they had something that many people, including ministers, do not have today. One important gift they had was the gift of preaching. They went around everywhere preaching the gospel.

They also had the power to work miracles, to heal the sick, and the list goes on. The day of Pentecost did not bring these gifts and miracles. They already had them and a lot more.

The Presence of God

What the Holy Spirit brought on the day of Pentecost was power and authority, and the focus of that power and authority was the exaltation of Jesus Christ. Now that Christ had ascended into heaven, the Comforter had come and given them the power and authority to exalt Jesus Christ. Jesus himself said, "And I, if I be lifted up from the earth, will draw all men unto me" (John 12:32). The Holy Spirit brought to them the desire and the power to lift up and exalt the Lord Jesus Christ.

One of the first things that come to mind as I think of the day of Pentecost is that they had a sudden consciousness of God being actually present with them. Up to this point, they had walked in the presence of Jesus, and now that He was gone, there was emptiness in their lives. The Holy Spirit brought down on the day of Pentecost a sense of the manifest presence of God in their lives that was richer than anything they had experienced when Jesus was with them.

They now had a fellowship with God that was so intense and so real that it changed their lives.

What is lacking in many churches and Christians today is this sense of the actual presence of God. Yes, we believe in God. Yes, we trust Him as our Savior. But for some reason it does not go further than that for many. We need to get back to the apostolic mindset that only the Holy Spirit can bring into our lives and realize that God is not only with us, He is in us and manifesting himself to us.

I cannot think of anything else that could change our churches today more than a sudden enduement from on high, resulting in the manifest presence of God in our midst. What would happen this Sunday morning if the Holy Spirit manifested Jesus Christ in such a way that people truly experienced His presence? That is the kind of revival I believe we need today.

Joy

Another thing that impresses me as I think of that early church is that even though they were going through some trials, suffering, and persecution, there was a sense of joy in their lives. Their joy did not come from what they were doing, it came from who was with them—the Comforter. They were true Christians, and they had the power of the Holy Spirit in their lives. There was an awesome manifest presence of God that lifted them above their circumstances and created in them joy unspeakable and full of glory (1 Peter 1:8).

I have been in some churches where there was everything but joy. Excitement, yes. Enthusiasm, yes. But the joy of the Holy Ghost was nowhere to be found.

We sing of joy in our congregations today. We often talk about it. But experiencing that joy is something altogether different.

What I hear is complaining; things are not going right. Their circumstances are other than what they would like. All of this complaining seems to take away the real focus of the Christian life, which is Jesus Christ.

In Hebrews, it says, "who for the joy that was set before him endured the cross . . ." (12:2). The joy of the Lord was not connected to His circumstances. And if we really have the joy of the Lord, it can never be compromised by situations or circumstances in our lives.

The early church got together, sang joyfully, and expressed their joy unto the Lord. It was not the happiness of the Adam nature, but the joy of the Christ nature.

Conviction

Another interesting thing about the early church after Pentecost was a new sense of power in their witness. Their words seemed to penetrate to the very heart of the people they were talking to. We sometimes call that conviction. Conviction is a work of the Holy Spirit. Because the disciples were filled with the Holy Spirit, the Spirit was operating through them, and He was able to convict people of their sin.

We have a whole culture in the church today that wants everything *but* conviction. You get a little negative with them, and they are out the door looking for another church that can soothe their sore spot!

We will never get anywhere unless the Holy Spirit has the authority to convict us so that He might bring us into a saving relationship with Jesus Christ and a steady walk with Him. The disciples in the early church spoke with authority, and their words penetrated the very heart of the people they spoke to.

Today people want to talk about having a good time, being the best person they can possibly be, how to be successful in everything they do. That was not the message of the early church. Their message was of such a nature that it brought conviction of sin.

Separation From the World

Another thing about the early church worth meditating on was a sharp separation between them and the world. In fact, the world refused to associate with the church because of the convicting power being exercised among them. There was absolutely no compatibility between the church and the world in those early days.

Why is it today that the world is very comfortable in the church, and the church is quite comfortable in the world?

There is no separation. A worldly man is willing to give an hour on Sunday morning to guarantee him a trip to heaven when he dies, as long as the rest of the week he is in charge of his life.

The early church knew a distinct separation from the world. There was no confusion about whether something was of the church or of the world. They were not looking for some big shot out in the world to say something nice and positive about the church. They would have none of that.

Prayer

The church in those days also took great delight in prayer. They met for prayer almost every day. Today, the contemporary church gathers for dinner. The early church gathered for fasting and prayer, which may explain the difference we see today.

Prior to Pentecost, the disciples said, "Lord, teach us to pray" (Luke 11:1). You never find that question in the book of Acts and afterward. Prayer was an automatic exercise for those in the early church. Nothing delighted them more than gathering together for prayer. They were praying people, and not only were they praying people, God worked through their prayers. In other words, they knew how to pray and what to pray for. Today, people pray for things that do not really matter one way or the other. The early church members understood the dynamics of prayer.

If we are to have a revival today, and I pray for that sincerely, I believe it will begin in the area of prayer. Once today's Christians have gotten beyond the mundaneness of amateur prayer and begin to take it as seriously as the early

Christians did, things will begin to happen as they did back in those days.

We often applaud a man like George Mueller, who was definitely a man of prayer. His whole ministry was built upon prayer. I do not believe George Mueller should be an exception in today's church. We all should be like George Mueller in the area of prayer. Do we believe in prayer as the early church did? Do we understand how God works through our prayers? When we begin to get back into the prayer form of the early church, we will begin to see God working in ways that will bring joy and praise into our hearts.

Love for the Word of God

One last aspect of the early church that I want to emphasize here is their love for the Word of God. I would remind you that in the early church they did not have personal copies of the Scriptures. First, the New Testament had yet to be written. But they loved the Scriptures. And as the apostle Paul wrote letters to the churches, they embraced them, and the Holy Spirit began to use them.

I think if we are going to have a Spirit-filled life, we need to have a deep love and appreciation for the Word of God. Those early Christians embraced the Bible, and it cost many of them their lives. If you read down through church history, you will find many believers lost their lives because of their devotion to the Scriptures.

The early church understood the place of the Holy Scriptures, not only in their own lives but in their church life as well. What place does the Bible have in our lives today? What place does the Bible have in our worship services?

Complete Surrender to the Spirit

All of this and more shows the difference the Holy Spirit made in the early church. If we are going to allow the Holy Spirit to be who He is in our lives and in our churches, we will begin to see some of the characteristics of the early church become the characteristics of our churches today.

I encourage people everywhere to begin believing that the church can once again be the church as it should be. The only way for that to happen is a complete surrender to the Holy Spirit. The Holy Spirit is not just a doctrine we ascribe to. The Holy Spirit is not just part of the Trinity. The Holy Spirit is the One who is to come into our life and the life of our congregations and bring the power and authority of God himself. For the Holy Spirit to work in my life, I need to surrender all authority and all power to Him. For the Holy Spirit to work in our church life today, we need to surrender absolutely to the Holy Spirit.

Now, the question is simply this: Will we allow the Holy Spirit to make a difference in our lives and in our churches today?

Blessed Holy Spirit, may You be welcomed in my life and the life of my congregation. Manifest Yourself to the glory of God our Father. Amen.

REFLECTIONS

Think of the last time you were convicted about something.

What was the outcome of that conviction?

Describe moments of God's manifest presence in your life.

A Portrait of the
Spirit-Filled Church

Behold, how good and how pleasant it is for brethren
to dwell together in unity!

—Psalm 133:1

I must confess I enjoy admiring paintings of the great
Masters. Whenever I am in New York City and have
the time, I visit some of the museums to look at these
grand old paintings. I especially love the portraits.

In examining these wonderful portraits, a thought oc-
curred to me: *All those portraits are composed of hundreds,
maybe even thousands, of brushstrokes.* However, when I
look at that portrait, I am not conscious of a brushstroke.
My focus is not on one brushstroke, but on the whole picture.

A great painting comprises many strokes in harmony, or
blended if you please, making individual strokes disappear.

The beauty of color is that there are basic colors available to everybody. But there are unlimited combinations of these colors, enabling the artist to create something unique that only he can create. That is why some of these old paintings are worth millions of dollars. We can separate the colors in our thinking, but not in reality.

Everything in the picture is in absolute harmony. If something sticks out, it destroys the focus of the painting.

Every Spirit-Filled Church Is Unique

Such can be said of the local assembly, a Spirit-filled church.

That is, every Spirit-filled church comprises the same basic ingredients, but it is the mastery of the Holy Spirit to make each congregation unique in and of itself. Each congregation is not a cookie-cutter reproduction of some other congregation. If that happens, a denomination is in trouble.

I believe every Spirit-filled church will reflect this aspect of the Holy Spirit. I grant you that the Holy Spirit is much more than we could ever comprehend. There are certain things about Him we can understand, things He has revealed about himself in the Word. But there is a lot more that we have not yet discovered about the Holy Spirit.

It is in the setting of the local church that the Holy Spirit does His best work. Nowhere else can the Holy Spirit be seen better. That is why the Spirit-filled church is so crucial in our day and age. The church started in apostolic times with Spirit-filled congregations and nothing has changed to disqualify that. Although I must acknowledge that many so-called congregations are not Spirit filled. Many congregations are simply "man filled": guided, directed, and empowered by men.

I believe a Spirit-filled church will reflect the beauty and harmony of the Holy Spirit. It will be an unlimited beauty, growing year by year and generation by generation. It is in the Spirit-filled church that the Holy Spirit delights to reveal himself and do the work He is longing to do.

As I have mentioned before, every local congregation is different in a variety of ways. But what I want to focus on are the certain elements of the apostolic church found in every Spirit-filled church. The exterior may be quite different. Our buildings, of course, are different now. And I could go on about the differences between today's church and the church in the apostolic age. But all those differences are external and superficial.

Let me list several things that are true in a Spirit-filled church today just as they were in the apostolic church.

Unity

The first thing that comes to mind is that in the apostolic church there was a unity of fellowship. This is needed today, and can be found in a Spirit-filled church.

On the day of Pentecost, the Christians were united and were one in fellowship. The Holy Spirit did not create the unity, but the unity brought down the Holy Spirit. It was the platform in which the Holy Spirit could do His work.

What we have today in a Spirit-filled church is the supreme unity of the brethren. There is that which brings us together in oneness that cannot be explained by worldly methods or procedures. We do not come together because we are using business or entertainment methods. We come together because there is one thing we focus on, and that is the Lord Jesus Christ.

When we come together in this spiritual unity, we become the soil in which the Holy Spirit can begin His ministry.

Yes, many things are different about us as individuals. Even in the apostolic days, there were differences among believers. But we do not focus on the differences; we focus on what unites us.

The essential beginning of a Spirit-filled church is the unity of the brethren. This is not something we vote on. It is something we experience even before we walk into the church building. The building does not unite us. A denomination does not unite us. If these things are the uniting factor, then we have failed to understand what being one in Christ is all about.

Authority

Another element that is the same in every Spirit-filled church is the authority of the Holy Spirit. I will mention throughout this book the fact that many have neglected the Holy Spirit. They recognize Him as the third person of the Trinity, but the authority of the Holy Spirit in the life of the local church has been largely neglected today.

We have our own authority, our own agenda. We get together to form a vision and a mission statement, and then we are off to the moon. We have at our disposal all the elements of business, which we use to bring the church together.

But the Spirit-filled church recognizes and honors the authority of the Holy Spirit. They do not move or do anything until there is a stir of the Holy Spirit in their midst.

Going back to the apostolic church, we see the influence the Holy Spirit had on what they did and did not do. Read about the revivals in years past and realize that every revival resulted from a renewed authority of the Holy Spirit in the local church. They got on their knees and refused to do anything until there was a move of the Holy Spirit.

I have often said and will repeat it now: What is needed today is for churches to call a moratorium on all activity for six months, get together on our knees, and wait upon the Holy Spirit to move in the direction He wants us to go. I believe that if every church in America today would do that, there would be a move of the Holy Spirit equal to all the revivals we read about in the past. Only the Holy Spirit can do that.

The Exaltation of Jesus Christ

The third element evident in the apostolic church that should be found in every Spirit-filled church today is very simply the exaltation of Jesus Christ. I cannot stress this enough.

The basic work of the Holy Spirit in every congregation is to lift up Jesus Christ. It is the exaltation of Christ that identifies the authenticity of the Holy Spirit. Jesus said, "And I, if I be lifted up from the earth, will draw all men unto me" (John 12:32). The only legitimate person who can so lift up Jesus Christ is the Holy Spirit.

It is in the confines of the local church that the Holy Spirit lifts up Jesus Christ. Everything He does in that local church has this as its ultimate goal: to exalt Jesus Christ.

On the day of Pentecost, when the Holy Spirit came, there was such an exaltation of Jesus Christ, the whole church was pooled together in worship and adoration and praise. When the Holy Spirit has His authority and is allowed to do what He wants to do, His primary job will be to exalt Jesus Christ.

We have a generation today that wants to exalt people, or even programs. We want to exalt everything and everyone but the Lord Jesus Christ.

Of course, we use the name of Jesus in our prayers, hoping that will get us somewhere in our praying. We would say nothing negative about Jesus Christ. However, when we come to church, instead of exalting Jesus Christ, we exalt personalities, celebrities, and programs. Often this is what brings us together, which is a pseudo-unity that will never endure.

Such was not the case in the early apostolic church. There were no personalities, no celebrities, and no programs that united them. All they had was the Holy Spirit, and all He did was exalt Jesus Christ.

Today we need a renewed emphasis on exalting Jesus Christ. I know we cannot in our own strength exalt Him properly. Yes, we can talk about Him, preach about Him, and witness about Him. But the only One who can truly exalt Jesus Christ is the Holy Spirit. We will know there is the authority of the Holy Spirit in our congregation when there is an overwhelming sense of the exaltation of the Lord Jesus Christ in our midst.

Harmony of the Gifts

A fourth element I would add here is the harmony of spiritual gifts. It should seem most natural that the Spirit-filled church would experience a harmony of the gifts of the Holy Spirit. Only a Spirit-filled church provides the platform for the Holy Spirit to exercise and direct these spiritual gifts.

If it is a Spirit-filled church, one gift will not dominate in that church. Yes, there will be times when one gift will rise above another, but there will be a harmony and a unity of spiritual gifts in the church.

I will deal with this in another chapter, but I believe in all the gifts of the Holy Spirit. I believe they should all be present in the church today.

The thing about these spiritual gifts and the direction of the Holy Spirit is that they all focus on exalting the Lord Jesus Christ. Again, we come to the full picture. A great painting is not just one brushstroke. A great painting is the blending of colors and brushstrokes, giving a single focus.

In a Spirit-filled church, where the Holy Spirit is in charge, there will be a harmony of spiritual gifts, and out of that harmony will come a clear focus on the person of the Lord Jesus Christ.

Let me be very clear here when I say that spiritual gifts are under the authority and supervision of the Holy Spirit. They are, after all, the gifts of the Spirit. They are never at the discretion of any person, and they are definitely not religious toys to entertain us.

Great harm has been done in this area because good church people do not understand this whole matter of spiritual gifts. The gifts are under the absolute direction of the Holy Spirit. He picks a gift to exalt at any one time; it is up to Him and His leadership.

These four elements that were in the apostolic church are also in the Spirit-filled church today: unity, the authority of the Holy Spirit, the exaltation of Jesus Christ, and harmony of the gifts of the Spirit.

A Warning

I need now to give a warning. It is simply that a Spirit-filled church is the target of the Enemy. He knows the potential of a Spirit-filled church and that the focus of such a church is the exaltation of Jesus Christ, which the devil hates with a passion.

He starts his attack by undermining the work of the Holy Spirit. His key is to attack the unity of the brethren. If he can wriggle his way in and cause unrest and division in the fellowship, he is undermining the work of the Holy Spirit.

Disunity among brethren is the leverage the Enemy exploits for his purpose and agenda, which is to move the focus away from Jesus Christ. However and whatever it takes is what he is going to do. I hate to admit it, but he has been quite successful.

This is why Spirit-filled churches need to be focused on the Holy Spirit and the work of the Holy Spirit in their midst. Let us not get all caught up with a demonstration and exaltation of personalities or celebrities. Let us not take the spiritual gifts completely out of context, but rather let us submit ourselves daily to the authority of the Holy Spirit and allow Him to do what He wants to do.

Nothing is more beautiful than a Spirit-filled church displaying the marvelous harmony of the Holy Spirit in its midst.

Blessed Holy Spirit, I rejoice in how You have exalted Jesus Christ in my life. May I so live as to allow You to do this every day of my life. Amen.

REFLECTIONS

How would you evaluate your church with regard to the presence of the Holy Spirit?

Are you the kind of Christian who fits in a Spirit-filled church?

What are some changes you could make in your life to bring yourself into harmony with the Holy Spirit?

The Harmony
of the Spirit-Filled Church

And when the day of Pentecost was fully come, they
were all with one accord in one place.

—Acts 2:1

I f the Holy Spirit is what the Scriptures, the creeds, and
the hymns say He is, what does this fact have to do with
you and me? The best illustration, of course, is the early
church and the disciples. The platform of the Holy Spirit's
work throughout the early church was the harmony of the
believers. It all began with the disciples.

The Best Seminary

The disciples had three years of the best Bible school in the
world. Imagine a seminary equal to one with Jesus Christ

as the entire faculty. They did not get a framed degree to hang on the study wall, but they had a degree within them and they loved Christ our Lord. They loved Him when He was alive, they loved Him after He died, and they loved Him after He arose from the dead.

At this point, they had received nothing; they had only been promised something. Up until His death and even afterward, Jesus created a certain expectation in the disciples. He told them there was a new kind of life for them. It was not to be a poetic life, a psychic life, or even a physical life; rather, it was to be marked by an outpouring from above. It was to be something that would come down upon them out of the world beyond, over the threshold of their being into the *sanctum sanctorum*, into the deep where the Spirit lived, teaching them, instructing them, making them holy, and giving them power. Jesus would tell them of these things as He came near the end of His earthly life. He told them there was a new and superior kind of life coming; it was to be an infusion, an outpouring of the Spirit. And then He left them.

Being in one accord is a musical term that means harmony. The early disciples were already one. They were in harmony with each other. They all gathered together in one place. Someone has said that we have yet to see what God can do with us if He can get us all together in one place.

God Is Greater Than Words

Always remember, God is bigger than anything God can say because words are inadequate to express God and what He can do. Any promise that God ever made God has to *overfill* it—the reason being that God is so great, His heart so kind,

His desire so intense that language cannot express it. Neither Greek nor English nor any other language can adequately express God and His promises.

God promised the disciples they would receive power, and that power would come down from heaven upon them. What He did was cross the threshold of their spirits, enter into the deepest depths of their souls, and dwell there forever. He worked within them to lead them, purify them, instruct them, teach them, and help them understand that the fulfillment would be greater than the promise, because the fulfillment is God himself, and the promises are mere words. God is always greater than words.

The Error of Being Positive

There is a great modern error abroad, and you will find it out if you read me any length of time because I am not one of those positive preachers. We are told to be positive today, to accent the positive and underplay the negative. But everyone who knows how to screw in a lightbulb knows there is a positive to an electric circuit, but you cannot have a light burning on the positive alone. It takes both the positive and the negative.

A man is known by the enemies he makes. I want God's friends to be my friends. I want to be in harmony with them. But I am not so particular about whether God's enemies are my friends. In fact, I do not want to be friends of those who are enemies of God. Sometimes I need to tear into things I do not believe are right. I would not do it except that it hinders the people of God. Anything that hinders God's people is my business.

This harmony with the Spirit needs to be settled personally, because if I try to make you believe something, you will go away and meet a man who is a better arguer than I am and who will make you believe the opposite. If you can argue a man into believing he is filled with the Spirit, another man will argue him out of it. If you can argue a young fellow into thinking he is born again, he will meet someone who will argue him out of it. I never argue with anybody. I point to the Lamb of God that taketh away the sins of the world, and after that the man is on his own. Then, if I drop dead or get hit by a car, he will still have the promise of the Father, and he will not have to go back to me for assurance.

The reason I can talk about this with a good deal of authority is that I went through it, and I know what I am talking about. No one can say Jesus is Lord and believe that Jesus is Lord except under the influence of the Holy Spirit.

Harmony in the Gifts of the Holy Spirit

When we come to the gifts of the Holy Spirit as presented in the Scriptures, we will see there are varieties of them. In 1 Corinthians 12, the apostle Paul says there are various kinds of gifts but the same Spirit, various kinds of official services and yet the same Lord, various kinds of effects and yet the same God (vv. 4–6). Notice the Trinity here: the Holy Spirit, the Lord Jesus, and God the Father. The same God who produces all the effects in each person is a manifestation of the Spirit, and the gifts have always been granted for the common good (v. 7). The gifts of the Spirit create harmony in a Spirit-filled church.

Paul says to one the word of wisdom has been granted through the Spirit. Unto another the word of knowledge by the same Spirit, and to another special faith, and to another various gifts of healing, by the same Spirit, and unto another the exercise of miraculous power, unto another the gift of prophecy, unto another the gift of discernment between spirits, unto another the variety of gifts of tongues, to another the interpretation of tongues. However, all these results are brought about by one and the same Spirit, allotting to each individual as He pleases. Just as the body is one and yet has many parts and all its parts are many, they make up one body. So it is with Christ. In fact, in one spirit, all of us, whether Jews or Greeks, slaves or free men, are all baptized to form one body, and we are all endued with one Spirit. (See vv. 8–13).

The apostle Paul writes to a different group and says that to each of us individually His grace was given according to the measure of the gift of Christ (Ephesians 4:7). For this reason, Scripture says,

And he gave some, apostles; and some, prophets; and some, evangelists; and some, pastors and teachers; for the perfecting of the saints, for the work of the ministry, for the edifying of the body of Christ: Till we all come in the unity of the faith, and of the knowledge of the Son of God, unto a perfect man, unto the measure of the stature of the fulness of Christ: That we henceforth be no more children, tossed to and fro, and carried about with every wind of doctrine, by the sleight of men, and cunning craftiness, whereby they lie in wait to deceive; but speaking the truth in love, may grow up into him in all things, which is the head, even Christ.

Ephesians 4:11–15

So we shall no longer be carried about with every changing wind of doctrine, according to men's cleverness and unscrupulous cunning, making use of every shifting device that misleads. We shall lovingly grow up into union with Him who is our head, Christ. Dependent on Him, the whole body, its various parts firmly adhering to one another, grows by the aid of every contributing ligament and power portioned to each individual part, so it is built up in the spirit of love.

Harmony in the Fellowship

When Paul knew he was not going to be around for long and wanted to get everything straightened out, he wrote to Timothy: "Now the Spirit speaketh expressly, that in the latter times some shall depart from the faith, giving heed to seducing spirits, and doctrines of devils" (1 Timothy 4:1). It is obvious Paul was not well schooled in the art of not being offensive, or, as we say today, being politically correct. This is offensive language, but some are listening to deceiving spirits and the teaching of demons.

He continues:

Speaking lies in hypocrisy; having their conscience seared with a hot iron; forbidding to marry, and commanding to abstain from meats, which God hath created to be received with thanksgiving of them which believe and know the truth. For every creature of God is good, and nothing to be refused, if it be received with thanksgiving.

vv. 2–4

Paul was not married, but he determined that nobody was going to lay the yoke of celibacy upon anybody. If they wanted to marry, they could do so as far as he was concerned. He warned that they would have double trouble if they married, but it was their decision (1 Corinthians 7:28). Paul was a man, like so many, who loved to eat. He was frugal, carefully practicing fasting along with tears, but he was determined nobody was going to lay compulsory fasting on anybody.

Harmony in the fellowship is the key. When there is disharmony, it keeps the Holy Spirit from doing what He wants to do. Paul encouraged Timothy to be careful so as not to allow pseudo-doctrine to disrupt the harmony among believers.

Holy Spirit, I praise Thee and worship Thee for Thou alone are worthy of worship. Amen.

REFLECTIONS

Compare the harmony in our bodies to the harmony that should be present in the local church.

Think of some things that disrupt harmony in the church.

How can you protect yourself from this disruption?

The Holy Spirit: An Uncomfortable Presence

And they continued steadfastly in the apostles' doctrine and fellowship, and in breaking of bread, and in prayers.

—Acts 2:42

One issue that needs to be dealt with is simply *who would be uncomfortable in a Spirit-filled church?* I think this is an important subject because not everyone is going to be comfortable when the Holy Spirit is Lord of all.

Many think everyone is anxious for a move of the Holy Spirit in their church. They may say they are interested in it and are praying for it, but there may be nothing that suggests they would be willing to actually see the Holy Spirit move in their midst.

Controlling People

When dealing with the Holy Spirit, we are dealing with God. When we deal with God, we must deal with Him on His terms, not ours. Most people do not quite understand that, even some Christians. They believe God is at their disposal at the snap of their fingers.

This would be the first group of people uncomfortable in a Spirit-filled church. They want to be able to tell God what to do and when to do it. They may have good intentions—I do not argue that—but their intentions are not rooted in the Scriptures. Does not the Bible say that not all men have faith? When we come into a church setting, we must leave behind us our will and our intentions.

I will grant you there are many good people in the church, but they really do not understand who the Holy Spirit is and what He is about. Yes, they have heard teaching about the Holy Spirit. But they do not know the practical application of submitting themselves to the Holy Spirit.

Take some people's prayer lives. Their prayers are based upon what they want and when they want it. Even if what they want is contrary to the plain teaching of the Scriptures, they still want it.

These people will be very uncomfortable in a Spirit-filled church.

Sunday-Morning Christians

I think another group of people uncomfortable in a Spirit-filled church are those who put on their religion as a suit for Sunday morning. After the service, they carefully take off their suit and hang it up until next Sunday.

Those who want to walk with Christ day by day and moment by moment are not in this category and do not put on their religion like a sweater. They put it on as their garment for day-by-day living. If the Holy Spirit is going to move in my heart, I must commit myself to Him every day of the week with expectations based on Scripture.

Nothing in the Scriptures says the Holy Spirit will only move on Sunday. These people think Sunday is the time the Holy Spirit will move. If He does they are excited about it, but then come Monday morning it is a different story. We cannot tell the Holy Spirit when He is to move and when He is not to move.

Looking back at the history of revivals and the great movements of the Holy Spirit in our past, you will discover revival was never at the whim of the church. The revival was a work of the Holy Spirit in His time and in His way.

People who want to limit the Holy Spirit like this will certainly be uncomfortable in the Spirit-filled church.

Pleasure Addicts

There is another group of people in the church that would be very uncomfortable if the Holy Spirit moved in their midst. They are those who are addicted to entertainment and pleasure.

I must confess that there is nothing entertaining or pleasurable about the move of the Holy Spirit. When the Holy Spirit begins to move, He often uproots many things we have grown accustomed to. He destroys those things we have been resting upon in order that we might come to the point of resting wholly and completely upon Him.

Entertainment is not in the scope of the Holy Spirit. Many churches have given way to this attitude of entertainment and as a result have hindered the Holy Spirit from working.

People often come to church to feel good about themselves and have positive thoughts about where they are going and what they are going to do. As long as the pastor can soothe them and make them feel good about themselves, they are going to keep coming. The Holy Spirit does not work that way. Rather, the Holy Spirit will not soothe you, nor will He make you feel comfortable. The Holy Spirit may uproot your present life and bring a bit of discomfort to you.

As I have read biographies of those men and women involved in great moves of God in the past, I have noticed one thing about them. All of them have different lifestyles and different personalities; they are different from one another. The one common thing among them all was a disruption of their life. When the Holy Spirit moves, He disrupts a person's life. Those who do not want that will not be comfortable in a Holy Spirit-run church.

Along this line are people who really want church to be fun. They want church to be full of games and activities and fellowship, dinners, picnics, and you name it. If it is fun, they are going to be there. If it is a worship service where the focus is on the Lord Jesus Christ, chances are they are too busy to come. They will flock to a church picnic but will never show up at a prayer meeting.

We have a fun generation trying to run the church today, and these people will never be comfortable in a Spirit-filled church.

Big Shots

Another thing is true: A Spirit-filled church will never be a platform for people who desire to be big shots and popular personalities.

In order for the Holy Spirit to begin to work in the church, those personalities and celebrities need to die to themselves. The Holy Spirit will not allow them to run His church.

Yet this is what we see today. If the pastor is not a celebrity or vibrant personality he cannot draw a crowd. The crowd wants to go where the popular celebrity is. Worship has become our performance. The one who can put on the best performance is the one who is going to get the largest crowd.

These people would be very uncomfortable in a Spirit-led church because the Holy Spirit will never bow to a personality or celebrity. The Holy Spirit will always be God. And those who are looking for celebrities and personalities will be very uncomfortable with the exaltation of Jesus Christ.

As I have said before—and I do not mind repeating myself—the purpose of the Holy Spirit in the church is to glorify Jesus Christ, and He cannot be glorified when competing with celebrities and personalities.

The big shots are running the churches today. And if I may be so bold, I believe they are running them into the ground. These people would be very uncomfortable if the Holy Spirit took over the service on any given Sunday. They are in charge, and what they want to happen is going to happen. Their agenda is what is important, and they are going to work toward that agenda and point people in that direction.

Those Who Confuse Worship With Entertainment

I might as well get right to the point and include the area of singing here. The singing portion of church services— which some call worship— has spun out of control today. Our singing is on par with the world and the concerts the world puts on. As such, it fails to glorify the Lord Jesus Christ.

Those who think singing a hymn is entertainment surely will not be happy in a Spirit-filled church. I have had people tell me that singing a hymn is a form of entertainment. If it is, I will sing no more hymns as long as I live. However, I know differently.

Those who believe singing hymns is entertainment have not the first idea of what worship is all about. Worship is never about the person worshiping, but rather the Person we are worshiping. Is our singing today in the local congregation for our pleasure or is it to glorify the Lord Jesus Christ?

I believe that is the hardest question to answer, and yet I believe it needs to be answered. People who are convinced that singing is entertainment will never last in a Spirit-filled church.

When I sing, "Amazing Grace, how sweet the sound," I am worshiping God Almighty. To even suggest that that is a form of entertainment borders on blasphemy.

Those before the throne cry day and night without ceasing, "Holy, holy, holy, Lord God Almighty" (Revelation 4:8). If that is entertainment, then I am an entertainer; but I assure you, it is not. First and foremost, I am a worshiper. The church must worship, and worship and entertainment are at opposite ends of the table.

Spirit-filled worship will make some people very unhappy and uncomfortable, but Spirit-filled worship is what we need in our churches today. There is more healing joy in five minutes of true worship than in five nights of reveling. No one ever worshiped God and then committed suicide as a result of a hangover. Many a man has killed himself because he burnt himself out trying to have fun. Many a young woman goes out, throwing herself into having fun, and before she is twenty-five years old she is worn out.

Cultural Christians

There is another category to cover before I finish this chapter. Those who embrace religion for cultural value will certainly not be happy in a Spirit-filled church.

The church can become the center of the culture of a neighborhood. They want concerts, book reviews, picnics, and all sorts of things. This kind of thing happens frequently. But they really do not want a move of the Holy Spirit in their midst.

The local church becomes a place to better yourself, upgrade your business, or find a husband or wife acceptable in the community. These kinds of people will never feel at home in the church with the Holy Spirit in charge. They have completely different agendas.

If you look at these categories closely, you will discover very few people who would be happy and content in a Spirit-filled church. Perhaps that is why the evangelical church today is on a downswing. Those focusing on the work of the Holy Spirit are not going to have the crowds they once had. Those who do have the crowds usually are those offering the people what they want so they will come.

Blessed Holy Spirit, many do not welcome Your presence. I do, and I invite You to rule and reign in my life today and every day. Amen.

REFLECTIONS

Think of how a Spirit-filled church would affect your life.

Would any part of such an influence offend you?

What would you need to change personally to receive the Spirit's presence?

The Holy Spirit
at Work in the Church

> For the perfecting of the saints, for the work of the
> ministry, for the edifying of the body of Christ: Till we
> all come in the unity of the faith, and of the knowledge
> of the Son of God, unto a perfect man, unto the mea-
> sure of the stature of the fulness of Christ.
>
> —Ephesians 4:12–13

The definitive work of the ministry, which the saints are to do, is the edifying of the body of Christ, and not so much an ordained ministry. Every Christian has a work to do, and it is primarily the building up of the body of Christ.

How God Works

The question we need to explore is how God does His work, His final work, His eternal work. We need to understand how God is working if we are going to be used of God and the Holy Spirit.

I find in the Scriptures about four methods whereby God does His work in the church.

Consecration to Christ's Glory

The first method is by consecration of Christians to Christ's glory alone. We do not recognize mere performers. We do not believe God intends that performers are to come in, and we are to be a kind of religious stage upon which they may perform, take their bow, and then go off to the next performance. That is not God's way of doing things. We believe His way of doing things is through His people, not the brilliant people always, but the plain people like you and me. What the Bible so tenderly calls the common people.

Politicians in our day like to use the phrase *the common man*, and they do it for political purposes. Our trouble, of course, is that we have too many common men in Washington. Now, you can take that for what it is worth, but they say *common people* because they are political. The Bible refers to the *common people*, a dear term to God, and the common people always surrounded Jesus. He had some stars too, but mainly they were common people. The consecration of these common people to Christ and His glory is what God recognizes.

Prayer

Then, of course, we have the prayer of faith. Would I be asking you an embarrassing question if I asked when you had your last prayer answered? The prayer of faith should be a prayer that engages God, meets God's conditions, and then turns loose the power of the Holy Spirit.

Spiritual Gifts

The third method God uses is the exercise of spiritual gifts. The giving of these gifts and the exercising of these gifts is what the work of the ministry is all about. The gifts of nature are not enough. There are natural gifts that people have. Musicians have natural gifts. Sometimes those natural gifts can be used and we can enjoy them. They are good any place you put them, but you cannot do holy work that way. Only the Holy Ghost can do holy work.

The Power of the Holy Spirit

The fourth method, of course, is the power of the Holy Spirit. Only He can author any real, lasting work in the church. Nobody else can possibly do it. There must always be power present.

You no doubt have in your home a washing machine. If you put clothes into it with water and detergent, you can wash your clothes. Indispensable. There is a second thing that does an important work in the home, and that is the refrigerator. It is a great time-saver and extraordinary convenience. Then maybe you have a radio or a TV for news and entertainment. Maybe you have a space heater for the rooms that do not get quite warm enough. You can add any other appliance that makes your life easier. Electrical appliances are all built to do a certain work, but without power, they will never do any work. They must be connected to a source of power. And so it is in the work of God, in the church of God, we need power in order for anything to happen.

Without the power of the Holy Spirit in a person, whatever he does, he might just as well play somewhere else. So it is with a man who can speak, so it is with a man who can teach, so it is with everyone who may have a natural talent. The mighty Spirit of God has to animate and quicken and give overtones of creativeness or we do not have a church at all.

When the energizing of the Holy Spirit does any work, God's work, it is done in an everlasting way. God is very kind and tender, but He is very tough on the flesh. He is tough on carnality and proud flesh. Carnality and flesh cannot do the work because they cannot be injected with the power of the Holy Spirit no matter how talented a person may be or how much of a genius he may be.

That fact makes it very hard. It submerges the worker and the work, frustrates the carnal desire to give and receive honor, and starves the appetite for glory, which lies at the root of every one of us. If all you have to do is be "converted" and bring that desire for glory over into the church, you can spend a lifetime of religious work doing nothing but getting glory for yourself. When we finally understand that no human gifts, no human power can do the work of God, but that it must be the energizing work of the Spirit, the bottom falls out of all of our glory and all of our human pride. God gets all the glory and that is hard on the flesh. Any method man uses to carry on the work that is not spiritual, as I have named here, only feeds the flesh.

What the Church Should Aim For

You might say, "But what are you aiming at, Mr. Tozer? Are you going anywhere with this? Is there anything good the church is trying to do, or are we simply going around the religious merry-go-round, riding the wooden horse, holding on to the painted mane, round and round with a little musical accompaniment? Is that what we are here for?"

Answers to Prayer

Some people would think so, but I know a good deal better than that. For instance, we gather together because we believe it is the will of God that a company of people should meet in the name of Christ as an assembly of redeemed believers, and that among other things there should be marvelous answers to prayer. One miraculous answer to prayer would do more to help the congregation and to encourage it and cheer it up and cause it to lift up the hand that hangs down and strengthen the feeble knees than all the advertising you can do in the wide world.

The Presence of God

Therefore, we believe in the presence of God and we want nothing that disturbs or grieves that presence of God. If we knew we could have a hundred thousand dollars laid at our feet, we would not take it if we thought it would disturb or in any way grieve the gentle presence of God.

Revival Wonders

Then there are such things as revival wonders. When I was a very young preacher, I preached on revivals and how to have them. I have my old notes yet, but I learned that it is very easy to do, but very hard to make good on. What I mean by revival wonder is that within the church somebody suddenly enters into a new, grand, and wonderful spiritual experience. Let that happen to just one person and things begin to change.

Conferences and committee meetings are good, and I do not object to them. However, just let one person get filled with the mighty Holy Ghost, and the spiritual fallout will come to everyone around him. Just let somebody get blessed in some sphere, somewhere, and all around the circle everyone will be helped by it.

I do not believe that it can be superimposed, that it can be bought. I do not believe we can bring it in on an airplane or by freight. I do not believe we can get that, except as the Holy Spirit energizes His people.

Joy

Then, I believe in the joyfulness of the children of God. I am not exactly sure what might be called by nature an optimistic man—not particularly cheerful—but the joy of the Lord is still the strength of His people. I believe the sad world around us is attracted to spiritual sunshine.

Some churches train their people just the same as the Fuller Brush Company trains their salesmen. They teach them how to smile and show all of their teeth and all that sort of thing. When I go into a church and a man who has been trained to greet me greets me, I know I am shaking the flipper of a trained seal. But when the Holy Ghost is in the congregation, they are just spontaneously joyful and cannot keep it back. It has a wonderful effect on people.

Joy is desperately needed today. We have nothing to cheer us in the world around us. The world looks tragically bad, and all we hear from the radio and newspaper is about wars and cancer and heart disease, and job loss, and people are worried. Young people in high schools and colleges are worried because, they say, "What's the use? What is there to look forward to?"

Christians should be the happiest people in the world, and should not have to look anywhere but in the Bible and to God above for satisfaction and joy.

New Spiritual Experiences

I believe you can get a group of people who know how to reach God in prayer and get answers to their problems. They are the people who have had—some of them at any rate—a new spiritual experience, and it will show in their faces. I do not believe we need much more to prosper as a people of God.

Love

We need more love for one another. Granted, it is easy to love some people, and some only their mothers could love. Yet I am determined, by God's help, to love them. You can choose to love people. Love is not a feeling. It is action; it is doing, and the Lord says to love people. He did not say that we need to *feel* love for them.

Revival Music

Another good thing is revival music. God the Holy Spirit sings in a man or woman. Everything God ever did, He did to musical complement. Do you know that when He made the heavens and the earth "the morning stars sang together, and all the sons of God shouted for joy?" (Job 38:7). Do you know that when He led the children of Israel across the Red

Sea on their way finally to Palestine that they sang? (Exodus 15:1). And when Jesus went out to die, having sung a hymn, they went to the Mount of Olives (Matthew 26:30). When He rose from the dead, He said, "I will declare thy name unto my brethren: in the midst of the congregation will I praise thee" (Psalm 22:22).

According to all the traditions of the church, the prophecy of the resurrection of Jesus is in Psalm 22. He sang among them. Did you know that when the Holy Ghost came to Pentecost, it became a singing church? Did you know that every time there was a new poured-out blessing down through the centuries the people of God became the singing people?

Today we sing the songs born out of revivals hundreds of years ago. We are singing the revival of the Friends of God in the fourteenth century, the songs of the Moravians when they had their revival, the songs of Martin Luther of the Reformation revival, the songs of Charles Wesley at the time of the Wesleyan revival, and we are singing some of the Salvation Army songs of the time of the General William Booth revival. We have not had any new songs amounting to anything in recent times because we have not had a true revival.

If we can call down the blessing of God upon us, as we should, I believe there will be new songs written in our day equal to those written in other days to fit the things God is doing. It may be a reason for revitalizing and reactivating some of the old songs.

G. Campbell Morgan left his church in London to visit churches in Wales during the Welsh revival. They had great singing in his Westminster Chapel in London, but when he got back, he stood up and scolded the people. He said, "You've never sung in your life. I have just come back from Wales, and such singing you have never heard." They were singing the songs, but they were singing them with the buoyancy and lift that help bring people under conviction and to faith. This man of God saw the difference and wanted his own congregation to know about it.

I believe in joyful gospel singing, such as this camp song:

I WILL MAKE THE DARKNESS LIGHT

I will make the darkness light before thee.
What is wrong I'll make it right before thee.
All thy battles I will fight before thee,
And the high places I'll bring down.

Charles P. Jones

Words From the Pulpit

Lastly, there is the good word that sounds from the pulpit. I am not the greatest preacher of my day by a long shot, but my commitment is to preach the words of the living God from the pulpit. Every congregation needs to hear the books of the Bible expounded, the truth told, the text illuminated, and the truth illustrated from the stories of the Bible, until the Bible is everything.

You only have to have a big heart that wants the will of God more than anything else in the world, and a single eye to His glory. There are these things that matter: the Word of God, sweet music, answers to prayer, coming into the fullness of joy, sweet friendliness, words from the pulpit, personal interest in each other, and love for each other. These things matter the most.

When we exercise the gifts of God's Spirit energized by the Spirit, though we may not build big as the world sees it, we will build forever. That is what I aim for. I would not want a dime of money or a minute of your time if I could not guarantee you that you could build forever. I do not guarantee that you will, because motive is everything and I do not know your motive. But I guarantee that you can build forever by the grace of God, and you can do things that will be here long after you are gone. It is wonderful to leave something behind you after you are gone.

Holy Spirit, Thy leadership is absolutely essential in my life and in my church. I honor Thee by giving Thee full rule in my life. Amen.

REFLECTIONS

Think of the last time you were consciously moved by the Holy Spirit.

Do you remember some of the expressions of the Holy Spirit at that time?

How has your life changed as a result of the work of the Holy Spirit in your life and circumstances?

Standing in the Power of the Spirit-Filled Life

Ever learning, and never able to come to the knowledge of the truth.

—2 Timothy 3:7

Let me emphasize an important fact. We cannot live our Christianity in a vacuum. It is a complete impossibility. As Christians, we cannot enter into a glass ball, be suspended, have everything exhausted from it, and live our lives like that. We must live our lives in relation to something we call "our times."

The Times We Live In

Everyone has to live in relation to the times, including Christ, when He was on the earth, Paul, John, James, Peter, Luther,

Wesley, Knox, and down to the present time. No Christian ever tried, if he knew the Word of God and was not ignorant of it, to live in disassociation from the times in which he lived.

Now, the phrase *our time* or *our times* was used by Christ and by His apostles. The word *times* refers to a condition prevalent at any given period. We familiarly talk about hard times, and Christ Jesus our Lord repudiated the religious leaders because they did not know the times in which they lived (Matthew 16).

It is quite significant that He turned His back on these sign seekers. These Pharisees and scribes were the religious leaders of their day and wanted miraculous proof that Jesus was who He claimed to be. Our Lord rebuked them sharply by saying,

> When it is evening, ye say, It will be fair weather: for the sky is red. And in the morning, it will be foul weather to day: for the sky is red and lowering. O ye hypocrites, ye can discern the face of the sky; but can ye not discern the signs of the times?
>
> Matthew 16:2–3

The signs were all around them—moral, religious, and political signs of the times, and yet they demanded Jesus perform some miracle as proof that He was who He claimed to be, the Son of God.

For some time, I have wanted to share an apostolic warning. I do not like it. I wish it did not have to be here, and I think you will bear me record that I write and speak on this very rarely, perhaps not frequently enough.

In these days, preachers are told they should hurt no one's feelings, they should remember to be cultured and in sync with our times. I want to point out that Paul's illustration in 2 Timothy 4:3 is taken from no more fragrant a place than the swine pen. They had a disease in those days that pigs got, making their ears itch, and the only way they could get any relief was to go to rock piles and vigorously rub their ears against the rocks. Paul, this learned man who is said to be one of the six great intellectuals of all times, thought the only proper illustration about the last times would be pigs that have this disease that made their ears itch. He said they all heap to themselves teachers because they have itching ears.

That is what Paul said, and he gave us a preview of some "times" in 2 Timothy 3. I wonder if they could be these times. He said, for instance, "Men shall be lovers of their own selves" (v. 2). I ask you to notice whether these refer to times of selfishness? I ask you whether these are times of boasting? Paul is talking about the church now. He is not talking about the world. Paul is not fooling around with the world, but the church, the religious world. He says there are boasters these days. Then he said they would be disobedient to parents, lovers of pleasure more than lovers of God, having a form of godliness, but denying the power thereof (vv. 2–5). You decide whether these are of our times or not.

Then Paul said they are "ever learning, and never able to come to the knowledge of the truth" (v. 7). We are printing more Bibles than ever in the history of the world, publishing religious magazines more than ever; there are more Bible schools, seminaries, and colleges than ever before. Ever learning, yet somehow never seeming to come to the knowledge of the truth. They will not endure sound doctrine, the doctrine that is sensible; they want to spice it up. Itching ears, with religious leaders willing to scratch them, and turning doctrine into fables.

Whatever we deem our times to be, you can be sure they will become worse.

Let me tell you as a Christian, conditions are going to worsen before they get better. Christians are deceiving themselves by intensified activity and increased publicity for religion. This is moving, growing, and increasing like a cattle stampede; it grows by invitation and by the intoxication of success.

A philosopher once said that there are some things by which the more skillful you are the worse person you are. The intoxication of success is the imitation of those who point to success as proof that they are right. But success in a wrong thing only proves that the man is more wrong than if he failed, and it is because he can skillfully do wrong.

Then there is the encouragement of the crowd. There is nothing that makes a little boy bigger quicker than crowds. Take a tiny little man and surround him by a crowd, and by that peculiar psychological osmosis, the power of the crowd leaks through the thin hide of that little henpecked brother and for a moment, he is a big man because he is surrounded by people. It is the same psychology as a little fellow with big glasses getting into the big car his dad bought him, taking the muffler off, and roaring around the corner on two wheels. He somehow manages to gather from those roaring cylinders something of its power. What does he not have in himself that he gets from that engine? I pity such a man, and I can only hope that the day will come when he will be able to stand on his own two feet and not have to borrow power from a machine.

Responding to the Times

In these times, we as a church can do one of two possible things: We can be opportunists, taking our cue from the leaders of the world, and sacrifice eternal values for temporal success. (I have been around long enough that you know what I am going to do, God help me.)

The other option is to go into the mount, get our instructions, and come down, recognizing who we are and maintaining the character of a called-out assembly, a disinherited minority. Like Noah, our beliefs, our morality, are disinherited and rejected, but we can maintain our character and get into the ark. We can ride on top of the water; we can be in relation to what is around us but not drown in it.

What is our relationship to the world? The same as Noah's when his ark took on the floodwaters. He could not escape the times. He floated on the boiling, seething waters of judgment, but not a single drop entered that ark. It floated clean, and there remained that separation between the people of God inside and the brackish waters below.

So we can think of ourselves in that way. We are "a royal priesthood, a holy nation, a peculiar people" (1 Peter 2:9).

We Are All Priests

I believe in ministers and in ordaining ministers. I am not against them. But I am saying that the ordained minister is not the only priest. All the people of God are priests and a royal priesthood, including the simplest and humblest one reading this now who would think this the least applicable to himself. If you are a true Christian, you are a priest of the Most High God as surely as any minister or bishop. And we can think of ourselves as a company of priests. We need not go to a priest to get our entrée into the presence of God. We are priests, every one. We can enter into the presence of God without the mediation of any earthly priest.

God gives certain gifts, and the church has traditionally taken those gifts and recognized them and called men out, laid their hands on them, and said, "We believe this man is gifted of God, and that he will ably preach to us and lead us." That has been traditional in all denominations, and I am for it and believe in it. Let us not, however, pick one man out and say, "This gifted brother whom we now ordain to the ministry is our priest. The rest of us are followers." No, not by a long shot. Every Christian has as much entrance into the presence of God as the most famous preacher who lives in the world today.

Standing in Power

Some things we must stand against, and not only when it might be convenient for us or when it might call attention to ourselves. We must not smile at the altars of Baal. God gave to me nearly thirty years ago a verse along this line: "Thou shalt not bow down to their gods, nor serve them, nor do after their works: but thou shalt utterly overthrow them, and quite break down their images" (Exodus 23:24).

Someone who has been on his knees before an idol for forty years will not take kindly to someone kicking the idol over and breaking it. "Watch it," he says, "you've disillusioned me." But wouldn't it be better to be disillusioned now, while you have the time to do something about it, instead of waiting until Gabriel blows his horn?

The things we are against do not constitute our creed. Our glory does not lie in breaking idols; our glory does not lie in opposing things. The Scripture says, "Ye shall receive power, when the Holy Spirit is come upon you: and ye shall be my witnesses" (Acts 1:8 ASV). That power means the ability to do, not destroy.

Power is a positive, not a negative word. When Jesus promised His church power, He meant, of course, that they were to have power to stand against evil, but that was not the primary purpose. The primary purpose was that they should have the power to do good. The man who tells the truth has to stand against a lie, but is not conscious that he is standing against a lie. He is only conscious of telling the truth. The woman who is honest in her business stands against dishonesty, but is not conscious of standing against dishonesty. She is conscious of being honest. The teenager who is decent must stand against indecency, but he does not congratulate himself because he is standing against indecency. He stands for decency, and that is his power.

The Bible gives us the power to do and to witness. We are to tell what we have seen, heard, felt, and experienced. It all centers on the person of Christ. "Ye shall be my witnesses." A witness is someone who was there and tells what he saw. A witness is called to the bar of the court and put on the witness stand. He is asked, "What did you see?" If he says, "I didn't see anything, but my mother-in-law told me," they will dismiss him in three seconds. They do not want to know what his mother-in-law told him. What did you see? What did you hear that night?

Replacing Baal

The Christian has no right to smash someone's idol. I may be misunderstood here, but I would rather worship Baal than break down someone's false idols and never worship Jehovah. A false prophet who does not know Jehovah has no right to call anyone to Mount Carmel. Elijah was able to give them something better, and remember that is when the four hundred prophets of Baal were put to confusion and everybody cried, "Jehovah, he is God; Jehovah, he is God" (1 Kings 18:39 ASV).

The emphasis was not upon the destruction of Baal, but upon the discovery of Jehovah. No man has a right to break another man's idol unless he has a true God. No man has any right to stand against something evil unless he has something good to put in its place. No person has any right to criticize someone who is going the wrong way unless they are going the right way themselves and are willing to witness to that.

We are in a place where we are so pressed in from all directions. Almost everywhere we go, we run into old Baal somewhere, and we sit on our hands and react. I believe we have a message that is the biggest news in the world without apology. I believe we have a God who can meet any need, anywhere, and we need not kneel before the learned or before the world or any of the religions of the world. We do not need to kneel before the psychologist who is supposed to know all that goes on inside our heads. We need not kneel before anyone but the One who has risen from the dead, sits at the right hand of God the Father Almighty, and wears the only crown there is. He is Lord of heaven, earth, and hell. He is Jesus Christ our Lord.

So you and I have to demonstrate something. It does no good to talk about how bad evangelicalism is if we have nothing to put in its place. Say, you do not like what I am doing. You do not like what I believe. All right, what do you have? Do you have something to give me in place of what I have?

The church that has great grace upon it can break idols because they have something to put in their place. For us to take a stand and have no great grace on us, and no great power on us, is to put ourselves in the position of the seven sons of Sceva. They told the devil to come out of a man and the devil turned around and said, "Jesus I know, and Paul I know; but who are ye?" (Acts 19:15).

So may God help us. We are not only against something, but for something. Or we are against something only because we are for something better. And what we are for is so infinitely better than anything we could possibly be against that 95 percent of our message and thought and prayer should have to do with what we are for.

Holy Spirit, Thou hast established in me the truth of Thy Word. May my life be a proclamation of that truth to the world around me. Amen.

REFLECTIONS

How have you stood up for your faith?

Have there been any consequences of aligning your life with the truth?

Search your heart. What or who are you really for?

The Fruit of the Spirit Sustains the Church

But the fruit of the Spirit is love, joy, peace, longsuffering, gentleness, goodness, faith, meekness, temperance: against such there is no law.

—Galatians 5:22–23

There are moral ends after which the church of Christ seeks, for which Christ died and rose again, to which the Holy Spirit works here on mankind. It is to produce in human character all the attributes of the Holy Spirit: love, joy, peace, longsuffering, gentleness, goodness, faith, meekness, and temperance. These qualities are found in the Holy Spirit.

You know how it is in the sky above in the daytime. The sunlight comes down as a sort of solar light, a little on the gold side and yet with the whiteness that is not gold, but is the normal light we are familiar with all over the world. A piece of glass shaped in a certain way with light passing through it shows that sunlight is not one light, but many up and down the prismatic scale. We start with visible light and go down the scale to light waves that are so long you cannot see them. In a prism we can see about seven colors, the colors of sunlight.

God calls himself light and it is said that Jesus Christ is the Sun of Righteousness (Malachi 4:2) and God is likened unto Him. God is a sun and the shield (Psalm 84:11). The Holy Spirit is the Spirit of the Father and the Son together.

We sing, "Holy Spirit, light divine, shine upon this heart of mine, chase the shades of night away, turn my darkness into day" (Andrew Reed, 1817). Just like sunlight, the Holy Spirit is one, but when He comes into the human heart, He is broken up. You can see the character of the Holy Spirit broken up into sections, into colors, so to speak, as light passing through a prism. The qualities that the Holy Spirit would bring are these: love, joy, peace, long-suffering, gentleness, goodness, faith, meekness, and temperance. I want to look at these fruits individually, although they are of one essence and you cannot have one without the other.

Love

The Scripture says that the fruit of the Spirit is love. I think all the world would agree that love is the one thing missing today. You cannot pick up a newspaper, listen to the radio, hear a political debate or a debate on education or scarcely anything else without hearing antagonism, hostility, and hatred. The world is filled with hatred while God is love.

Now, how do we transfer from the God who is love into the bosom of the man who is full of hate the quality that is our loving God and let it shine and produce love light in the human heart? This problem God set for himself, but it is a problem that God, being the Almighty and the All-Wise, can and does solve. He sends the source of love to the human bosom. The Holy Ghost sheds the love of God abroad in our hearts, as illustrated in this hymn:

DOWN IN THE VALLEY, AMONG THE SWEET LILIES

Down in the valley, among the sweet lilies,
Walks my Beloved, his footprints I see;
Haste I to follow thee, Savior and Lover,
How the winds whisper thy dear name to me.
H. M. Bradley

How could we Christians be as we are—so cold, so bothered, our brows so furled? We ought to be men and women in love. Everybody knows that the person in love is a transformed person. The poor, crazy, debased world sings about it in a sultry voice, but they are right. As actor, singer Al Jolson wrote, when a human being is in love, it's like "there's a rainbow around my shoulder."

Now, as quickly as we can, let us go to that higher, holier quality we call the love of God.

I wonder how we could be as self-collected as we are, self-possessed, when we ought to be men and women in love. The love of God is in our hearts by the Holy Ghost. We love God and then we love others for God's sake. It seems to me as

Christians filled with the Holy Spirit, we will not only love God supremely but we will love everything that God loves for God's dear sake.

Everyone knows that when you have children in the home you love the little things the children love. If it is a rattle or a toy or stuffed animal, we love it because and only because the child loves it. So it ought to be of the things God loves.

Joy

I like to refer to the fruit of joy as joy power. People talk so much about joy, but we do not have the joy of the Lord.

I am becoming more convinced that the reason evangelical Christianity has so many carnivals and music shows and films and funny gadgets and celebrated men and women is that they do not have the joy of the Lord. A happy person does not need very much.

I heard a preacher on the radio recently say, "You can't defeat a happy man." The man who has the joy of God in his heart cannot be defeated. He has something inside that bubbles up. We do not have to try to create it. I think even God must get very sick of what He sees: all the little gadgets and trinkets we have to try to create a little happiness when we are simply missing the fountain of joy that only springs from within. When the well of joy is not flowing, then we try to paint the pump to get a little joy. We put jingle bells on the old pump handle, but it does not bring up the water.

Joy is something you cannot create. It comes from the Holy Spirit; it is one attribute of the Holy Spirit that floods the believer on a daily basis.

Peace

Then we have peace power, the peace of God in the human breast. God's people are not a peaceful people. I find so many people with wrinkles in the middle of their brows. Why? Because we are troubled. The world troubles us. We are troubled by business, troubled by everything around us. The Word of God says that the fruit of the Spirit is peace, and we habitually sing about things we do not have:

WONDERFUL PEACE

Peace, peace, wonderful peace,
Coming down from the Father above!
Sweep over my spirit forever, I pray
In fathomless billows of love!
Warren D. Cornell

We sing it with our knuckles tight and our brows drawn, worried about what will happen twenty minutes after we are out of church. We have worried ourselves out of peace instead of having peace by the presence of the Holy Spirit.

Longsuffering

There is power in longsuffering. Longsuffering is a disposition that bears injuries patiently. Not injuries that come from bruises, but injuries inflicted by the injustice of other people. People are to blame, certainly, and that is why we need longsuffering.

A synonym of longsuffering, of course, is patience.

You know how we Americans are—men and women anxious at the yellow light, ready to put a nickel in the slot, pull the handle down, and when we get nothing, kick the thing. An American is one who is impatient when he misses one opening in the revolving door.

Impatience brings on all our physical troubles and nervous troubles, and the Spirit of God counters that by giving us longsuffering. The difference is, He does not say to cultivate longsuffering; He says that the fruit of the Spirit is longsuffering. The whole thing cannot be cultivated, and I have tried to be faithful about that. I have endeavored to point out that there are certain gifts and talents, but there are some that come like fruit, and the tree does not cultivate the fruit; the farmer does.

Look at the vine. The husbandman cultivates the vine, but the vine does not cultivate itself. The vine cultivates nothing; the vine simply holds still and bears the fruit. The sap, the juice from God and nature working in the vine, produces the quality of the grape. It is something that the Spirit of God puts in our hearts (see John 15).

Gentleness

Then there is gentleness. Now, the opposite, of course, is harshness. Gentleness is an indisposition to injure anyone. It is the opposite of severity, and how are we going to have it in this terrible day? I do not know any way to cultivate it. It is only by the blessed Holy Ghost.

Goodness

Goodness is two things; it is virtue and kindness. The opposite would be unkindness or cruelty. So the Spirit of God brings to the believer that which is morally good, pure, clean, and honest, that which is useful to the moral life and to the heart.

Faith

The Holy Ghost produces in us faithfulness. If Christians were filled with the Holy Spirit, there would not be much backsliding. Why is there backsliding? Because people cannot keep their minds made up to serve God. You cannot simply give in to serving God by listening to a rapid-talking inspirational speaker or somebody that pulls on your heart-strings until you say, "Yes, I accept Jesus." If you can be argued into the kingdom, someone else can argue you out of it. If the Spirit of God does not open the door, illuminate a man, and lead him in, someone else can lead him out. The Spirit of the Lord comes in and produces in us faithfulness, steadfastness, and loyalty.

Faithfulness is implanted by the Holy Spirit. We are completely dependent upon the Holy Spirit; we have nothing He did not give us. Christ has been gone from the earth since AD 33 and is not back yet. He is at the right hand of the throne, and He in His visible human presence has not appeared in our day. He said, "I will pray the Father, and he shall give you another Comforter" (John 14:16). And this Comforter "shall teach you all things, and bring all things to your remembrance, whatsoever I have said unto you" (v. 26).

There has not been an advance in the church that the Spirit did not cause. There has not been a revival the Spirit did not bring. There has not been a success on the mission field the Holy Spirit did not give. There has not been a man converted whom the Holy Spirit did not convert. There has not been a Christian blessed whom the Holy Spirit did not bless. There has not been a prayer answered that the Holy Spirit did not do it. There has not been a Christian filled with the Holy Spirit whom the Holy Spirit did not fill. We need to get on our knees and spend at least fifteen minutes apologizing to God Almighty for the way we have treated the Holy Ghost.

Teachers have led us astray by telling us that He, the Holy Spirit, will not speak of himself and therefore we ought not to speak of Him. Do they not know that when the Scripture says the Spirit will not speak of himself, that it means He will not speak on His own behalf? It does not mean that He will not speak about himself (John 16:13).

Let me give you some rhetorical questions: Did the Holy Spirit inspire the Bible? If the Holy Spirit inspired the Bible, does the Bible speak about the Holy Spirit? If there is something in the Bible about the Holy Spirit and the Holy Spirit wrote the Bible, then did the Holy Spirit speak about himself? He did speak about himself. So when it says, "He shall not speak of himself," our teachers say, "Hush, hush, don't talk about the Holy Spirit. He does not talk about himself." The fact is He does talk about himself.

The Holy Spirit inspired Paul to say that everything that can be known about the Holy Spirit, the Holy Spirit himself teaches. Everything that can be known about Jesus, the Holy Spirit teaches, and everything that can be known about the Father comes from the Holy Spirit. Everything that we can know about theology the Holy Spirit provides (1 Corinthians 2:13–14).

An old German writer used to say that the heart is the best theologian. I like that. A heart filled with the Spirit, where the Spirit is illuminating the heart, is always the best theologian. You can always have more light than merely being taught by people, and I believe in being taught by people. Either I must learn through a long, hard process, or the Holy Spirit must illuminate me. Give me the man whose heart is illuminated by the Holy Ghost every time. You will learn more doctrine, more truth, more about the Bible in one flash of the Holy Spirit than you can learn in ten years in school. The Holy Spirit himself is a theologian, and He teaches us.

Meekness

Meekness, of course, is the opposite of arrogance. Meekness is softness of manner. There is not much of this in the day in which we live. We have breathlessness: Turn on the radio, and the speakers are breathless. Religious programs, particularly, arrive at a run and bounce along at a speed no Christian should ever try, breaking through the sound barrier. But softness of manner; only the Holy Ghost brings softness of manner.

A reader might stop and say, "Listen, Tozer, how can a man like you talk about graciousness and softness of manner?"

Well, if God had not changed my heart, do you know what I could do? I could cut the throat of a congregation and use nothing but my tongue. The Holy Spirit has made the difference in my life. It is not me trying to be meek, but it is my allowing the meekness of the Holy Spirit to have dominance in my life.

Temperance

Then there is the power of temperance. Temperance, or self-control, is the opposite of intemperance. The Holy Spirit is masterful in helping us control self. "You shall receive power when the Comforter comes" (see Acts 1:8).

Power to produce by God's power, in the loveless heart, oceans of love and in a joyless heart, fountains of joy. In a troubled heart, ponds of peace. To the impatient should come longsuffering. To the harsh person, gentleness. To the unclean, purity. To the unstable person, stability. To the arrogant, proud person should come meekness. To the intemperate person should come self-control.

If that is what we mean, I ask, who can rise up and criticize anyone? Who can say, "Tozer is a fanatic"? Is it extreme to say that a man ought to be loving and joyful and peaceful and faithful and meek and in control of himself? Is that fanaticism? If it is, O Lord, send more fanatics our way. Who is there, I say, that dare accuse us of fanaticism? Who dare say that we are fanatics when we say that the qualities that belong to God can be transferred by a mighty baptism of the Holy Spirit to a person and that person's character can be changed?

The Holy Spirit can transform you, change you, and make you holy inside. Anyone who says it is not so does not know the Word of God.

When the Holy Spirit comes on a person, the fruit of that presence will be manifest through his life. Fruit not produced by the person, but by the Holy Spirit within exalts Christ.

Holy Spirit, fill my life with Thy blessed fruit and nourish my spiritual life that I might glorify Thy nature. Amen.

REFLECTIONS

Meditate on the fruit of the Spirit as manifested in your life.

How has your life changed in regard to the expression of fruit of the Spirit?

Has this change influenced your relationships with others?

Spiritual Gifts: The Function of the Local Church

The Spirit of the Lord is upon me, because he hath anointed me to preach the gospel to the poor; he hath sent me to heal the brokenhearted, to preach deliverance to the captives, and recovering of sight to the blind, to set at liberty them that are bruised, to preach the acceptable year of the Lord.

—Luke 4:18–19

The church is the body of Christ, with Christ as the head. True Christians are parts of the body, and the Holy Spirit is to that body what our soul is to our body. The Spirit in the body gives to it life, cohesion, and consciousness. Each member recapitulates the local church, that is, every Christian is an illustration of the church.

The Body of Christ

Illustrations and parallels break down, particularly when they come to the sacred and infinite things of God. For a person's body to function, it has to be in one place. If you separate and scatter him around, he is dead. But the body of Christ does not all have to be in one place because its unity is the unity of the Spirit. Therefore, the church is never all in one place; some are in heaven and some are here on earth. The Holy Spirit, who is the life of the body, holds the body of Christ together. Each local group has all the functions of the whole group and sums up all the offices and illustrates the entire church of Christ.

The members, according to Paul, are each designed for a function. The eye is designed to see; that is what it is for. And the ear is designed to hear; that is its function. The hand is designed for many purposes. The foot for another purpose. Lungs for another purpose. The heart for yet another purpose. So all the parts of the body have their particular and unique function and are designed to cooperate and act in concert with one another.

Somebody might say, "Well, this is a pep talk," because actually it can all be summed up like this: All for each other and each for all. That is what Paul is saying here. He says that the whole body exists for its members, and the members exist for the whole body, and therefore God gives gifts that the body might profit withal (1 Corinthians 12:7). Remember one final thing: All the parts take direction from the head.

Cut the head off a person's body and there is no direction anymore.

Spiritual Gifts

These functions Paul talks about are the various functions and abilities the Bible calls gifts—gifts according to the measure of faith and gifts according to grace. Paul states, "Having then gifts differing according to the grace that is given to us, whether prophecy, let us prophesy according to the proportion of faith" (Romans 12:6). And, "But covet earnestly the best gifts: and yet show I unto you a more excellent way" (1 Corinthians 12:31). And also, "Wherefore he saith, when he ascended up on high, he led captivity captive, and gave gifts unto men" (Ephesians 4:8).

In 1 Corinthians 12:8–10, Paul says there is a diversity of gifts and then names nine of them. We say these are the gifts, but if you read the rest of the Scripture and what Paul says in the passages before us, and then what Peter says, you will find that there are more than nine gifts. There are about nineteen, and I have marked down seventeen of them here. But reading over in Ephesians, we come to two more: evangelist and pastor. Maybe in saying there are nineteen, I have counted too many because it is possible that some are synonymous with each other.

For instance, say you have a family member named Billy, and you also call him Willy. If you were naming your family members, and you said both Willy and Billy, you would have one too many because Billy and Willy are the same person. If you are counting the gifts of the Spirit as revealed in the New Testament, and if you should, by accident, find that the

Spirit has designated one gift by two names, then you have to cut it down and say, that is a synonym. But the number of gifts is not as important as knowing their purpose and function in the church.

Now, here are the gifts as found in 1 Corinthians 12:8–10, 28; Romans 12:6–8; and Ephesians 4:11.

Apostle

First is the gift of an apostle. When they hear this word, most Christians think of the twelve apostles appointed by Christ. Judas by apostasy fell away, and Matthias was added to make up the number of the twelve. Paul was called an apostle, but after that the office was not perpetuated. Revelation speaks of the "twelve apostles of the Lamb" (21:14). The word *apostle* is not only a name. It is a designation. It means an ambassador or a messenger or one commissioned to go out. It may be proper and permissible, if we know how we mean it, to call a missionary an apostle because they minister cross-culturally, and we hear Paul called the apostle to the Gentiles.

Prophet

The second gift is that of the prophet. Now, the gift of the prophet in the New Testament was only secondary to the gift of prophecy. In the Old Testament, the gift of the prophet was mainly to foretell events and to warn, to plead, and to call back every person to God. But in the New Testament, the gift of the prophet is not so much to foretell events, since the Bible has been written and the prophecy stands, and all the events have been foretold that God wants to foretell. The gift of prophecy in the New Testament is to

150

tell forth and to see with an anointed eye unto due season. Not simply to be a foreteller, but to tell forth what God has to say about a different time.

Teacher

Then there is the gift of the teacher. Not everyone can teach; we might as well admit that. Even among those who teach, few can really teach. There is a gift of the teacher, both a natural gift and a gift of the Spirit.

Exhorter

An exhorter is not so prevalent in our day, but the old Methodists were wise enough that they had an office of an exhorter. They commissioned him and called him a lay preacher. He was not licensed, could not marry people, could not officiate the Lord's Supper, but he could get up, preach against sin, and tell how wonderful God was better than most preachers can do. It might be interesting to remember that it was a lay preacher and exhorter who won Charles Spurgeon to the Lord.

Ruler

Now, the word *ruler* is used in the same sense as a ruler of the synagogue. He is not a legal ruler; he is simply someone who sets some direction and reads the Scripture and teaches. I do not know whether he might be synonymous with the pastor or not.

Other Gifts

Of course, other gifts dominate the church and are used by the Holy Spirit in His work. In this category, there are the gifts of wisdom, knowledge, faith, healing (which a few people have), miracles, tongues, interpretation of tongues, discernment, ministry, and helps (whatever that is I do not really know, but I think some people are gifted just to be helpers).

A person with the gift of mercy appears to be someone who is particularly gifted by the Holy Ghost to go about helping people who are discouraged and helping the poor and comforting the mourning and otherwise going about doing good as it was said of Jesus.

The gift of governments might be the same as the gift of ruling.

Next, there is the gift of giving. Somebody says, "Are we not all to give?" Yes, we are all to give. Just as we all are to have some wisdom, but there is such a thing as a gift of wisdom. We are all to have some discernment, but there is such a thing as a gift of discernment. We are all to show mercy and be helpful, but there is such a thing as a gift of helping and showing mercy. So, we are all to give, but there is such a thing as a gift of giving. I believe God enables some people—if they will allow Him by the Holy Spirit—to control and run a business and to be able to support the church and the cause of missions and the cause of Christ on earth, and help the poor in a way that the average person cannot possibly do.

There is also the gift of the evangelist, and the gift of the pastor.

These are gifts given by the Holy Spirit to individual persons. Just as the gift of sight is given to my eye, the gift of hearing to my ear, the gift of smelling to my nose, the gift of taste to my tongue, and the gift of manipulation to my hand, particular gifts are given by the Holy Spirit to every member of the body of Christ.

Human Talents vs. Spiritual Gifts

The work of the church is to be done by the Spirit through these gifted members. In the judgment—when we receive rewards for deeds done, and we know as we are known, and that which is chaff and that which is straw and stubble is separated from that which is gold and silver and diamonds, and all the bad of the flesh perishes and passes away, and that which is of the Spirit alone stands—you will find that not only does God design us to do all His work through gifted people, but *He does all His work through gifted people.* Of course, not all religious activity is done through gifted people, because not all religious activity is God's work.

This represents the difference between human talents and spiritual gifts. Many do not know the difference, and fewer still separate the two.

You do not have to have the gift of the Holy Ghost to be a preacher or a Bible expositor. We can become Bible expositors by reading commentaries, going to Bible school, and learning what people say is true of the Scriptures. A preacher gets up and preaches and a politician gets up and preaches. You only have to be able to talk and know how to use religious phrases to be a preacher. But in order to preach so it will stand in the day of the fire, you are going to have to preach by the gift of the Spirit. Any preaching not done by the gift of the Spirit is not true preaching of God. It is written that Jesus Christ was anointed of the Holy Ghost and went about doing good. He said, "The Spirit of the Lord is upon me, because he hath anointed me to preach the gospel to the poor . . . and recovering of sight to the blind" (Luke 4:18). Even our Lord Jesus Christ worked by a gift of the Spirit on His human nature.

You may be giving and serving and working. But if it is not by the gift of the Holy Spirit, you may lose everything you have, and everything you put into it may go down the drain in that day. If we do not have the gifts of the Spirit, then the church is thrown back upon five things, which I want to name.

Talent

I use the word *talent* for somebody whistling through his teeth or somebody who has a marvelous gift for impromptu composition of poetry. Someone else is marvelously gifted in mathematics. You can give him a whole handful of numbers, toss them up, and by the time they fall, he will tell you the sum of them. Now, those are talents. Some people are talented composers; some are talented musicians; some are talented singers; some are talented talkers; we might as well admit that. Often talent alone runs the church today, not the gifts of the Holy Spirit as God intended.

Psychology

Another method religion can carry on with is psychology. Many people have mastered psychology; they are amazing in how they handle people with mental and emotional issues. So the church can be run by psychology. The new pastor comes, and the crowd comes in, and the first thing you know you have what looks like an amazingly successful church, but that pastor is simply a shrewd psychologist who knows how to say "Jesus" in the right places and can say tender things that people like to hear.

Business Methods

Other religious work can be done by business methods. Much of church work is being done in this manner today. I really do not have to expand on this. Some know how to run a church like a good business and are successful at it, at least from the world's standpoint.

Political Techniques

Some use political techniques quite successfully. They are great negotiators. You give a little and I'll give a little and we will meet in the middle somewhere. By the time you get through negotiating, you have something other than what you started with.

Sales Methods

Along with political techniques come sales methods. A good salesman can make a good profit. When you bring sales methods into the church, you are depriving the Holy Spirit of what He wants to do and the way He wants to do it. Good salesmanship is convincing people to buy something that sometimes they do not even need—or want.

And so Christianity can be carried on by the exercise of human talents without a church of the Holy Ghost, by sharp use of psychology without a touch of the Holy

155

Ghost, by business methods, by political techniques, and by sales methods that have not one gift of the Holy Ghost in them.

When this takes place, we may not know it until the great and terrible day when our deeds are burned with fire, when only that which was by the Holy Ghost stands. Jesus said even now the axe lies at the root of the tree and whatever is not of God, was not planted by our Father, and does not bring forth His good fruit shall be cast down (Matthew 3:10). Much of the religious activity through the centuries has been activity wrought by talent and psychology, business methods, political techniques, and sales methods.

Now, I say we have the gifts of the Spirit in the church; every church ought to have them.

I do not know of a group or denomination or fellowship or communion anywhere in the world that fully realizes the Pauline apostolic doctrine of the body of Christ—with each member recapitulating the local church, and the local church recapitulating the entire church and working as a team, and each one having a proper gift as God gave them, and working thus in the Holy Ghost.

I know denominations and churches where there are a few like this among them. But I do not know of denominations or groups of churches where that is the regular and general and common thing. Each one of us can receive an outpouring, an enduement of the Holy Spirit, and when He comes, He invariably brings these functional graces, which will enable some to have sharp discernment.

Someone might say, "What gifts do you think we ought to expect?" First Corinthians 12:31 says, "Covet earnestly the best gifts." We have our right to pray for these gifts and covet them before our God, that we might use them to bless His church and glorify His name.

You ask then, "What are the gifts you would say are the most needed in the church today?" I believe the gift of discernment is number one on my list. Evangelicalism has ruled out the Holy Ghost and has gone blind in these decades, so the church has traveled over into entertainment-ism, rationalism, and worldliness. The true church of Christ is scarcely to be found anywhere on the face of the earth. Not because people are bad, but because people have ruled out the Spirit, and so the gift of discernment is not there, the gift that can discern what is needed and what is false.

If this gift of discernment had been in our leadership we would not be where we are today in the church. We would not be locked up behind dispensationalism, entertainment-ism, and something else over there, but we would be in the middle, moving along in growth. My prayer is that the leaders of the church today might be endued with the gift of discernment.

I believe we also need the gift of faith. Everybody has to have some faith or he would not be saved, but there are those who have a peculiar gift of faith.

I also think the church needs to have a few people with the gift of showing mercy. We are all so starry-eyed and long-distance in our piety. We tremble about unreached people on the other side of the world, but there are people within the neighborhood who could use a little help. I think the gift of mercy would be a great help in the local church.

God will not do anything for a church that He would not do for any other church. He will not do anything for a people that He will not do for any other people. And He will not do anything for anybody that He will not do for you. We can receive now the power of the Holy Spirit. "Ye shall receive power" (Acts 1:8), said Jesus about the Holy Spirit. When the Holy Spirit comes, remember this: You will have the power to do everything God has called you to do.

Holy Spirit, I praise Thee that Thou canst work through someone such as me. May my life be open for the working of Thy gifts to the glory of God. Amen.

REFLECTIONS

Think about how the gifts of the Spirit are operating in your church.

Is there a spiritual gift that is particularly needed right now?

What is your spiritual gift or gifts?

The Gifts of the Spirit Are Essential to the Church Today

> But covet earnestly the best gifts: and yet show I unto you a more excellent way.
>
> —1 Corinthians 12:31

My concern in this book is to stir up an interest about the great need of the gifts of the Spirit to come back into the church. I am not the only one saying this; it is being echoed and reechoed all over the world. God is saying the same thing to many other people around the world in every denomination.

When God wants to do a thing, He does not start in one local place. But He says the same thing to various people in different parts of the world and they find and know each other and begin to harmonize. What I say about the gifts of the

Spirit is not a private view of a little man who does not know his way home after midnight. It is the conviction arrived at by vast numbers of persons of the evangelical persuasion in many parts of the world and among many denominations.

The gifts of the Spirit in the church today are not only desirable but absolutely imperative. It is extremely necessary that we should have the gifts of the Spirit in the church, and let me show you why.

Unredeemed Bodies Need the Spiritual Gifts

In this new creation Christ Jesus is the head, the church is the body, and individual believers are the body's members. The old Adam fell and God wrote across him "mortality and temporality": You must die and you must go. But the new Adam came and died and rose and lives in order that He might be the Head of the new creation, which has not upon it temporality but perpetuity, not the mark of death but the mark of life forevermore.

Believers are yet in their unredeemed bodies. Whether it is the sweetest saint who kneels in prayer or the newest convert who has blundered into some mission somewhere and is saved, every believer has an unredeemed body. Now, it is perpetually redeemed, but is not actually redeemed. In case you might worry about my orthodoxy, read Romans 8:20–23:

> For the creature was made subject to vanity, not willingly, but by reason of him who hath subjected the same in hope, because the creature itself also shall be delivered from the bondage of corruption into the glorious liberty of the children of God. For we know that the whole creation groaneth and travaileth in pain together until now. And not only they,

but ourselves also, which have the firstfruits of the Spirit, even we ourselves groan within ourselves, waiting for the adoption, to wit, the redemption of our body.

You cannot operate through ungifted members. For instance, I have a pair of hands. They are about average, and I cannot play a violin; they are ungifted hands. I cannot paint a picture; they are ungifted hands. I cannot play an organ; they are ungifted hands. I can barely hold a screwdriver, and I am getting worse as I get older. If I had to screw something somewhere at home to keep the place from falling apart, I would be in trouble since I do not have gifted hands.

We slow God down in His working because the gifts of the Spirit are not present. They are the organs through which the Holy Ghost does His work.

Ungifted men can do religious work, but it is only the human mind doing a human work; it is only a mortal mind doing a mortal work. In every work man does, whether building a church, or writing a hymn or a book, or promoting a movement, or playing or singing or organizing, no matter what he does, it is only a mortal doing a mortal job. All across it God will write, "It came to die," and "It came to go." Mortality and temporality are written all over the church of Christ today because men are trying to do in the power of the flesh, that is, in the power of their own genius, what only the Holy Ghost can do. Genius cannot do an immortal work. Genius can only do a mortal work, and do not be fooled by the loose use of the word *immortal*.

I do not say that God cannot take a handsome man and work through him, but He will not work through his handsomeness. I do not say God cannot take a man with a dynamic personality and work through him, but He has never used his dynamic personality. He will work through that, beneath that, and beyond that, but He will never use that. The Holy Ghost does not need it.

What does the mighty Holy Ghost, whose breath brought the world into being, need of your bright eyes and curly hair? What does He need of your fine voice? He does not need it. This is awfully humbling. We like to be able to retire and have people come around and say, "Look at all this man has done." If he did it, it will die. If he did it, it will pass away. But if he was a humble organ through whom the Holy Ghost worked, it will live and last and time cannot wear it out because it will have the qualities of deity in it. "Thou remainest, O God, Thou remainest" (see Hebrews 1:11).

Assembled religious people, well fed, coffeed up, and in a comfortable room with other men and women and a good musical instrument, can move in the flesh. That is like a mouse eating his way into cheese, thinking it is heaven. Christians are eating their way into the kingdom of God: "Come, believe in Christ, and let's go eat."

The work of God does not depend on good social spirits. It is the eternal Spirit working through gifts, which He has imparted, which are also eternal, to do an eternal work. Anything that falls short of it is simply religion and nothing more. When it is the work of God, He gets the honor, and man stands reverently with his head bowed and says, "Thine be the glory, forever and ever, amen."

The critical need in the church today is that the church should have these gifts, these organs through which the Spirit can do His work. The gifts are rare, but there's never been a time when there were not a few of the gifts present somewhere in the church. There is a consecutive link upon link and chain of spiritual Christianity down through the years, showing that the spiritual gifts have always been present in the church, even sometimes among those who did not understand them or did not believe in them.

Who Has the Spirit?

The Scripture says, "Ye shall receive power [when] the Holy Ghost is come upon you" (Acts 1:8); "Be filled with the Spirit" (Ephesians 5:18); and "Covet earnestly the best gifts" (1 Corinthians 12:31). Paul never meant to say to the Corinthians what many evangelicals have made him say. He never meant to say that they were to choose between love and the gifts of the Spirit. Then he said, "In case you want to know what gift I think is the most important, I would rather that you prophesy" (see 1 Corinthians 14:1). And by prophesy he did not mean to foretell events. He meant that God would put in the heart, the body, mind, throat, and nerves of a person, a strange, beautiful ability that would enable that man or that woman to speak with an unusual quality of conviction and everlastingness. It may be a housewife, maybe a man who sweeps the streets, maybe a bishop, maybe an evangelist, maybe a humble pastor in some unknown country parish. Whoever it may be, he has an unusual ability to speak with conviction and inspiration that is not human but divine. The results, while they may not be vast, will be eternal and permanent.

Now, does everyone have the Spirit? Yes, every Christian has the Spirit. Paul says in Romans 8, "If any man have not the Spirit of Christ, he is none of his" (v. 9). Except you be reprobate, every Christian has a measure of the Spirit. In 1 Corinthians 12, we are told that "by one Spirit are we all baptized into one body" (v. 13). But in the same chapter where Paul explains this, he says, "I would not have you ignorant [about spiritual gifts] . . . but covet earnestly the best gifts" (vv. 1, 31). If the fact that we have a measure of the Spirit when we are converted was all Paul wanted us to know, he would have said that and quit. But he explains at great length that the Holy Spirit is the Christian's birthright. It is not only for the great, it is the birthright of the most humble saint.

First Corinthians 1:18–29 tells us the people who were Christians in those early days were simple people: "God hath chosen the weak things of the world to confound the things which are mighty" (v. 27).

What shall we do about all this? Shall we freeze up, hide, and say, "I'm not going to be fanatical"? We are stone cold. That is our biggest problem. It is not fanaticism we need to be afraid of; it is spiritual frost. What shall we do then? Bring your empty earthen vessel.

Bring Your Vessels, Not a Few

Are you longing for the fullness
Of the blessing of the Lord
In your heart and life today?
Claim the promise of your Father;
Come according to His Word,
In the blessèd, old time way.

Refrain

He will fill your heart today to overflowing.
As the Lord commandeth you,

"Bring your vessels, not a few."
He will fill your heart today to overflowing
With the Holy Ghost and power.

Bring your empty earthen vessels,
Clean through Jesus' precious blood.
Come, ye needy, one and all;
And in human consecration
Wait before the throne of God
Till the Holy Ghost shall fall.

Refrain

Like the cruse of oil unfailing
Is His grace forevermore,
And His love unchanging still;
And according to His promise,
With the Holy Ghost and power
He will every vessel fill.

Refrain

Leila N. Morris

Remember, to be filled with the Spirit is a most solemn, searching, and sometimes painful experience to go through. The Holy Ghost is not painful. He is the gentle love of God, but getting ourselves ready, getting cleaned up, poured out; confessing, getting forgiven, getting straightened out with people, getting restitutions made, that can be painful.

How to Be Filled With the Holy Spirit

How can I be filled with the Holy Spirit? There are three D's I want you to consider: desire, determination, and desperation.

The first, of course, is to desire above everything else to be filled with the Holy Spirit. You will never be filled with the Holy Ghost until you desire to be filled.

This desire must become all-absorbing. If there is anything bigger in your life than your desire to be a Spirit-filled Christian, you will never be a Spirit-filled Christian. If there is anything bigger in your life than your longing after God, you will never be a Spirit-filled Christian.

I had a lot of joy when I was first converted, real joy. I was a happy Christian, but to be filled with the Spirit, God emptied me of my joy and showed me that it was about half carnality. He wants to deliver you from disappointment and emptiness. Sometimes He lets people fall flat on their faces, and that shocks them because they thought they were better than that. No, you are not better than that. You just found out how bad you were.

Now, is the desire to be filled with the Spirit the all-absorbing thing in your life? Nobody was ever filled with the Spirit without first having a time of disturbance and anxiety.

You will never be filled with the Holy Ghost, even if you do desire to be, until you become determined to be.

Though you are determined that you are going to be filled, you will not be filled until, in desperation, you throw yourself into the arms of God.

I am talking now about the filling, the fullness, and the anointing of the Holy Ghost. I like the word *anointing* better than *baptism*, for I am not at all sure that theologically we are not baptized into the body of Christ when we are born again. The word that I want to use is *anointing*. Anointing is not a gradual thing. When they poured oil on a man's head, it was not gradual. They turned the vessel over and poured it out, and it ran down all over the beard, down to the skirts of his garment. Everybody a quarter a mile around knew he had oil poured on him because it was the oil of frankincense and myrrh and aloes and cinnamon and smelled up everything around with its beautiful fragrance. It didn't happen gradually. It happened instantaneously.

We cannot think our way into the filling of the Spirit. We have to close our eyes and make the leap of faith into the arms of God. After every trick and everything you know to move toward God has failed and your desperate heart cries, "Fill me now, fill me now," then you move into that zone where human reason has to be suspended for a moment and the human heart leaps across into the arms of God. Then human talent and human glory and human honor and human duty and human favor all go out into the darkness of yesterday, and everything is God's honor, God's glory, God's duty, and God's favor. You have been broken and melted before God.

Holy Spirit, help me to embrace Thy work through the gifts Thou hast established for Thy glory. Amen.

REFLECTIONS

How has the Holy Spirit made your Christian walk a blessing to others?

How do you nurture that walk each day?

Have you been filled with the Holy Spirit?

Our Personal Pursuit of the Holy Spirit

Can two walk together, except they be agreed?

—Amos 3:3

The Holy Spirit, being a personality, cannot be known in just one encounter. Our relationship with Him must be cultivated, and I want to explain how this is done. Yet I wonder whether anyone is ready for this. I doubt some are. Some definitely are not ready for a chapter on how to cultivate the Spirit's companionship for several reasons.

Not Ready to Give Up Their All

The basic reason is that people are not generally willing to give up their all for *the* All. The All is the Holy Ghost; the

All is Jesus Christ; the All is God the Father. The Trinity is not plural but singular.

The world is full of a variety of things. We fall in love with these things and get lost in the plural, whereas God is bringing us slowly to the singular. God is singular: God, the Father; God, the Son; God, the Holy Ghost; the triune God in unity; the three in One. And God is bringing us to this One.

We are holding on to the plural, to the many, and forgetting the One. We will not give up all these things in order that we might have All, which is not things but God. I am sure there are some who turn their faces two ways at once. We face both directions and think we can get something of the world and something of God, and that by walking the tightrope or the fence in between, we can manage to have a little of earth and a little of heaven. As we get older, we hope to shift a little and get more of heaven and less of earth until the time when we are about ready to die, when we'll have all of heaven and none of earth. That is the way many have it figured, and that is why some never strike oil, why they never know they have issues between them and Jesus Christ and why they are never filled with the Spirit. They are satisfied to have a little of this world and a little of the world above, and they are never quite ready for that final surrender. They are never ready to give up their all to get the All.

Christianity As Insurance

Many Christians want Christianity for its insurance value, just as they want any other kind of insurance. They believe in hell and want to miss it; they believe in heaven and want to gain it; they believe in the reality of their sin and want to escape the consequences of their sin; and they want to be guaranteed that when they die there will be a safe haven for them to go to. Christianity seems to be the only way, so they get Christianity for its insurance value. If I accept Christ, it guarantees I will go to heaven and not hell, and then it is finally all right with my soul. Many people are willing to support the church regularly and even generously because they consider it for its insurance value. They are even willing to go along and be a little inconvenienced by it. Who would not be inconvenienced by an insurance policy if it was very valuable to him? Therefore, we are willing to stop certain things and do certain other things, and we are willing to change our lives a little, not basically, just a little on the surface.

Social Christianity

Then there are those who are not ready for this because their concept of religion is social and not spiritual. They have watered down the strong wine of the New Testament until it has barely any taste at all and it is easygoing. They introduce their own easygoing opinion into it, and Christianity becomes one verse of Scripture, plus two verses out of their own head, and three verses out of the newspaper and four verses out of an Almanac and five verses out of a book they have read, and something Aunt Minnie told them. Christianity is a hodgepodge with a little of God—not very much—and not much of Scripture.

Many churches today exist for their social value. They are churches without any religion at all, who do not believe the Bible, do not believe in Christ as Savior, do not believe in God in any proper, definitive sense of the word, yet nevertheless manage to carry on. They build educational buildings and have thousands and hundreds of thousands of dollars coming into their coffers every year to keep up a social splendor, where their lives can be enriched socially, and that is about all.

You cannot tell anyone involved in this kind of church how to be filled with the Holy Spirit or how to cultivate the Spirit's acquaintance, because those people come to church for the social value alone. That is where the young fellow meets the girl, where the girl meets a young man; that is where old cronies meet, where they discuss their golf game, their politics; it is where the old ladies discuss who is engaged to whom and who is going to have a baby and whether this fellow is leaving his wife or not, and on and on. It is a social center with a little religion mixed in. Some say, "That isn't true of our church." You would be surprised how many people attend church for no higher reason than that. You would be surprised if God Almighty were to turn the X-ray on our hearts.

Distracted by Entertainment

Some are not ready to hear about how to cultivate the Spirit or how to be filled with the Spirit because they are more influenced by Hollywood than they are by the New Jerusalem. They are more influenced by a movie magazine than they are by the Scriptures. In their dress, in their looks, in the way they decorate, in their physiology, in their language, and in everything else, they resemble Hollywood and Broadway more than they resemble God and His people.

They are not Christians in any true sense of the word because they never let God do anything to them or with them. They never let Him change them or let any transformation

172

take place. They have accepted Him, they say, but that is all there is to it.

People will follow the soap operas on radio or television year after year, and all those soap operas are alike. I know they are always having difficulties, as if there were not real troubles enough in the world, and we have to pay for radio or television in order to introduce imaginary troubles to keep us all stirred up. Some people have not wept an honest tear for anybody in distress, but they will weep while there is somebody sitting at a desk somewhere in the studio making believe they are in trouble.

Jesus Christ did not come into the world to listen to imaginary troubles. He came into the world to save us out of real troubles, and if we Christians were what we ought to be, it would be the real troubles that mattered. The great preacher Billy Sunday told them in his day, "Some of you are babies. You haven't wept over the lost and depraved for God knows how long, but you'll go down to the opera and wipe your tears with your beautiful gloves, weeping over some old gal who's not in any difficulty, but is only pretending and playing a part." He had something there, and the same is true today.

Thrill-Seeking

I do not know why, but we want a thrill, any thrill. People want to be thrilled somehow or other, and there are those who want to be filled with the Holy Spirit and know the Holy Spirit for its thrill value.

Most want the thrill of it, but they do not want the holiness of it; they want the joy of it, but they do not want the purity of the Spirit-filled life.

Walking With the Holy Spirit

How can we cultivate the Spirit's acquaintance? "Can two walk together, except they be agreed?" (Amos 3:3). That, of course, is a rhetorical question, and the answer is implied in the question. Can two walk together, except they be agreed? The simple answer is no.

Now, if two are going to walk together, there have to be some major points of agreement. They are going to have to agree on their direction. If I say, "I'm going to walk today," you might reply, "I'm also going to walk today. Couldn't we walk together?"

I would say, "It depends on whether we're going the same way."

"Well," you say, "I'm going to walk east."

I say, "I'm sorry, but I'm going west."

We cannot walk together unless we can agree on which way we are walking. We cannot walk with the Holy Ghost unless we agree to walk the way He walks and go in the direction He is going.

In order to walk together, we have to agree on the direction but also the destination. We have to have a destination and say, "Now, I'm going to that same place, that same destination." If we cannot agree on the destination, then we cannot walk together.

We also have to agree on which path to take. If I am going to New York, there are four or five ways to get there. And if we are going to go there together, we are going to have to agree on one route and say, "We're going to stick together. We're going to go on the same route, not choose a different one."

It is entirely possible to reach China by going east, but it is also possible to reach China by going west. It all depends, of course, upon which way you would rather do it. Some of our missionaries sail from the West Coast in order to get to India and others sail from the East Coast and go over into the Mediterranean, down, and around that way to India. We have to agree on our route in order to travel together.

Then we must agree that it is to our advantage to go together. Some people don't make good traveling companions. So we are going to have to ask again, can two persons walk together?

We are going to have to agree on a direction, destination, route, and then whether we *want* to go together. Some people just do not want to agree to that; they are going to have to decide. They are going to have to decide whether they actually want to go the way the Spirit goes.

A Holy Way

In all seriousness, the Spirit-filled way must be a holy way. Some do not intend to clean up their lives, but they want the Spirit, and will wrestle all night to be filled with the Spirit. They will do many things to be filled with the Spirit, except clean up their lives. They do not want a *Holy* Spirit; they want a "holy" Spirit. They want a Spirit with a thrill, but if you emphasize the holy, they back out on you. They want the thrill of being a Spirit-filled person, but they do not want the Holy Spirit who makes their life holy. A Spirit-filled life must be a holy life, for the Spirit of the Lord is sensitive and is not going to dwell in an unholy life, a life that loves sin.

A man or woman who loves sin can have sin, but they will never at the same time have the companionship of the Holy Spirit. The Holy Spirit is holy, and He makes the place holy where He dwells. He does not require a holy place to come in, but He requires that you are willing that that place *should* be holy. After He comes in, He makes the place at His feet glorious. And whatever that means it must mean this: that wherever God lights down, that place becomes a glorious place. He makes the place of His feet glorious, and if the Spirit of God comes into our hearts, He is going to make that heart glorious, not necessarily dramatic.

Some encourage people to be filled with the Spirit that they may be widely known; get filled with the Spirit so they may preach like Spurgeon. The Holy Ghost never yet came to a person to make him famous or to make a celebrity out of him. The Holy Ghost never came to a man to give him a reputation. The Spirit of God comes on a person to make them holy, to gift them and enable them to witness.

Some want to be filled with the Holy Spirit so they can be another Billy Graham. No, you can only be filled with the Spirit if you are willing to be nobody, unheard of, unknown; walking in the quiet back ways of the world, in the shadow of other great people. When you walk in their shadows, they get the praise and you get overlooked. You will never be filled with the Spirit of God in order to be somebody, for the very desire to be a celebrity, the very desire for publicity, the very desire to be known abroad, the very desire to be great cancels out all the work of God.

Paul said there was power in what he said, though he spoke not with smooth, eloquent words, but with plain, blunt language that anybody could understand (1 Corinthians 2:1–4). But I believe the greatest gift in all the wide world is a meek and docile heart. Do you want that? Would you rather have that than be famous? Would you rather have that than be great? A meek and quiet heart is in the sight of God of great price (1 Peter 3:4).

The Spirit Tames Us

God finds us like the wild donkey, our nostrils wide and our eyes blazing and our ears laid back, hating the touch of leather, hating the touch and smell of people. The Holy Ghost comes, takes us over, and starts, as we say on the farm, breaking the colt. After that, the whole nature of the animal changes. He perks his ears up and whinnies when he sees you coming. His eyes are calm now. Lay your hand on his neck and he will lean over and nuzzle you. He understands "Giddyup!" in every language. You can let your kid go out and play with him without harm; he has been domesticated. The Spirit of God wants to do that for you. He wants to domesticate you, humble you, and make you meek. The Christian who has been transformed by the power of the Holy Spirit into a docile, obedient, meek, trustful person has more treasure than all the wealth of the world. Not all the gold in Fort Knox could compare with the wealth that comes to a man or a woman who has been tamed, broken, domesticated, humbled, sweetened, and "meeked down," as the Quakers say.

Oneness With the Spirit

There must come a oneness with the Spirit of God: one in our outlook, one in our hopes, one in our thoughts, oneness with the Spirit of God. I cultivate His acquaintance and His fellowship by oneness with Him.

Back in pre-Elizabethan days, they talked about being one with the Holy Ghost. An anonymous author wrote a book called *The Cloud of Unknowing*, and in that book, he said something to this effect: "I only want those to read this book who want to be one with the Holy Ghost, united, made one; made out of two, one; identified; a holy spiritual union."

You cultivate the Holy Spirit's acquaintance, first, by being one with Him and surrendered to Him, understanding Him as He does you, wanting to go the way He goes and wanting to be the way He is, wanting to be like Him. Gaining the advantage in the kingdom of God comes from knowing Him and seeking meekness. Many people are not ready to hear this word. They have never come to all this. They have never decided two can walk together, but when we do find that out, what a difference it makes.

Our Pilgrim fathers knelt on the bare rocks and worshiped God. We must not take for granted the price they paid for this freedom. We must also be spiritual people: We must know God, we must cultivate God, we must make His acquaintance, we must be filled with Him, and then we must go on in intimate fellowship with Him.

Holy Spirit, I embrace Thee for Thyself alone. May Your presence overshadow me and hide me in that secret place. Amen.

REFLECTIONS

What is hindering your relationship with the Holy Spirit today?

How much and what are you willing to give up in order to follow the Holy Spirit's leading?

Is your relationship with the Holy Spirit growing?

18

My Daily Walk
With the Holy Spirit

It is of the LORD's mercies that we are not consumed, because his compassions fail not. They are new every morning: great is thy faithfulness.

—Lamentations 3:22–23

No book on the Holy Spirit can ever exhaust the subject, and this book is no exception. A series of books could not exhaust the subject because the Holy Spirit is of such a nature that the more we know, the more we do not know.

I want to pursue this Holy Spirit every day of my life. I want my walk to be in complete harmony with the Holy Spirit. This has been the challenge of my life and will be until the day I graduate from this life into the next. Then I will pursue Him even more and with better equipment.

Throughout this book, I have tried to outline my convictions about the Holy Spirit. I have tried to be as careful as I can to back everything up with the Word of God. If you find anything in this book that does not square with the Word of God, you have the obligation to throw it out. Nothing we say about the Holy Spirit should in any way contradict the Word of God.

I might stress here the fact that nobody can really understand the Word of God apart from the Holy Spirit. I will touch upon that shortly.

Since my introduction to the Holy Spirit so many years ago, I have made it a priority in my daily life to get to know the Holy Spirit and to cultivate a relationship with Him that is personal and experiential. It is one thing to know about the Holy Spirit; as I have stressed in this book, it is quite another thing to know Him by personal acquaintance.

Everybody knows the president of the United States, but very few people know the president by personal acquaintance. And so it is with the Holy Spirit.

There have been about seven aspects of my daily walk that have kept me in pursuit of the Holy Spirit. Allow me to outline them here, and I trust something might speak to your heart.

Walk Slowly

The first thing that has been very important to me in my Christian walk is to walk slowly and not get ahead of the Holy Spirit. People today are in too much of a hurry to get nowhere.

When I first became a Christian, and then when I first encountered the enduement of the Holy Spirit, I started at a full gallop. I did not know very much, and I knew I did not know very much, and I wanted to find out as much as I possibly could. I had a thirst for knowledge that became almost an obsession with me.

As I began to mature in my Christian walk, I began to see the danger of such a thing. I began to see the danger of getting ahead of God in my life.

I learned to give the Holy Spirit all the time He needs to do whatever He wants to do. Being the kind of person I am, I have been guilty of giving instructions to the Holy Spirit as to how I think He ought to work and the timetable He ought to be committed to. I must confess this has not worked.

My thirst for knowledge is not slowing down, but I have been able to pace myself in this area. For example, when I first started reading my Bible, I tried to see how much of the Bible I could read in one day. If you have tried that, you know how that ends.

Now, instead of reading the Bible at a full gallop, I patiently and meditatively read the Word of God. I will not leave a verse until I have saturated my soul with that verse. My purpose in reading the Bible is not to read the Bible, but to encounter the Living Word. I have said many times, if you have read the Bible and have not encountered the Living Word, you have not really read the Bible.

Some people believe in speed-reading. I must say I do that with many other books, but I have learned not to do that with the Bible. In some books, you do not need to read everything, but with the Bible, it is an altogether different ball game. I want everything the Bible has for me no matter how long it takes. I am willing to wait on God.

I need to allow the Holy Spirit the time to walk me through the Scriptures in order for Him to do in my life what He wants to be done.

Don't Trust the Experts

A second thing along this line is that I have learned not to trust the experts, especially in doctrinal matters.

Now, a doctrinal thesis is a good place to start, but it is only a starting point. Try to understand the Bible doctrine as the Holy Spirit has outlined it in the Scriptures, but then move on to the place of experiencing that doctrine in your personal life.

One of the old saints made the comment that if you cannot apply a doctrine to your personal daily life it is because you do not really understand that doctrine. The doctrine of the Scriptures is not the playground of theological sports. Some people know doctrine, but they have never experienced that doctrine in their personal lives.

I learned to search the Scriptures daily to discover what is really true. Yes, I believe in preaching and teaching doctrine. I do it all the time. But my preaching and teaching of doctrine does not stop at presenting truth. It must pursue that One who is the Truth. Any Bible doctrine not rooted in the Lord Jesus Christ is not understood correctly.

I have read the experts, and I encourage people to do so. But my faith does not rest upon the teaching of the experts. My faith rests upon a personal experience with God, and the Holy Spirit orchestrates that.

Do Not Be Afraid of Opposition

The third thing goes along with the former: I have learned not to be afraid of opposition.

When I was a young Christian, I read everything I could get my hands on, even books by atheists. I wanted to know why they did not believe in God. I wanted to know how they got to that place of dismissing God from their lives. Many a time I would finish reading such a book, put it down, and cry out to God, "O God, I can't answer that man, but I know You!"

For some reason we have the idea that we need to answer everyone, but I have learned that some questions do not deserve an answer. Many times people will pose a question only to set a trap, and unfortunately many Christians walk into that trap. I know, because I have done so quite a few times.

Opposition is not bad if I know whom I have believed. If I am going to believe the truth, I must expect opposition. If I do not get any opposition, I must examine myself and see what I am doing wrong.

Don't Be a Know-It-All

Another thing is, do not assume you know it all. I cannot answer for anybody else, but there have been times, quite a few, that I have assumed I know it all. If you have been there, you know the problems that presents.

Spiritual knowledge that leads to spiritual experience is a process. It is like walking down the pathway and enjoying the roses along the path. Every day I grow in my knowledge of the Lord Jesus Christ. What I know today is much more than I knew last year at this time. I think of the first year of my Christian experience; as a young person, I thought I knew everything.

The great joy of my life has been to learn new things about God and to experience new things in my relationship with God. No matter how much I know today, tomorrow will bring me something new about God, and I am anxious to discover the newness of God in my life every day. God's mercies are new every day, and discovering the newness of God's mercies is the great joy of my daily walk with God.

Avoid Nonessentials

This brings me to the fifth thing, which is not to get bogged down with nonessentials. As a young Christian, I was tempted to get all caught up in theological nonessentials. Which is the right mode of baptism? That is almost as bad as asking how many angels can dance on the head of a pin.

Which is the correct Bible translation? How often should we celebrate the Lord's Table?

I certainly was caught up in many of these doctrinal non-essentials, and it slowed down my discovery of God and His newness in my life.

Every time I get around those doctrinal hairsplitters, I cringe a little. We think we have boiled everything down to a doctrinal formula, and if you have the right formula, you are okay.

One of the great blessings in my life throughout the years has been reading the great mystics. I have suffered a lot of reproach from that because some of the things they believed were contrary to good evangelicalism. I was not so much concerned with the peripheral things they believed. I was mainly concerned with their relationship with God and how it motivated their lives on a daily basis.

Certainly there were a lot of things I would not and could not go along with. I considered those to be nonessentials, and their relationship with God to be the essential thing. I wanted to know what they knew about God and how they came to know it and how it changed their lives.

It is easy to get bogged down with nonessentials and flounder in the quagmire of mediocrity.

Allow the Spirit to Speak

The sixth thing that has been really important in my daily walk is allowing the Holy Spirit to speak to me.

I know this goes against the evangelical culture of our day. I know we have some people who stand up, quote a verse, then go and live their lives as they want to.

Whenever I hear a preacher go on like that, I slip out the back door, find a quiet place, and invite the Holy Spirit to come and speak to me. Just an open Bible and quietness before the Holy Spirit; and before long the Holy Spirit is moving in my heart and speaking to me. Nothing is grander in the Christian experience than the Holy Spirit speaking to you.

Now, some people will ask about the voice. I am not sure about that. All I know is the Holy Spirit begins to speak into my spirit and fills my spirit with such presence that I do not know if I am in the world or out of the world. I think I know a little bit about what Paul was talking about in this regard (2 Corinthians 12:2).

Every day I need to make room for the Holy Spirit to speak to me in such a way that my life is a testimony of His grace.

185

I know we can fall into some esoteric religious swamp and think we are hearing voices. I suspect the man who hears voices in his head. That is not what I am talking about here. I am talking about the Holy Spirit manifesting himself to me in that marvelous *mysterium tremendum* (tremendous mystery) that cannot be counterfeited in the world. I may not be able to explain it, but I definitely know when the Holy Spirit speaks to me, and that is the time for me to stop whatever I am doing and listen.

Give Priority to God's Word

One last thing would be to give priority to the Bible.

I am so over arguing about which Bible translation is the correct one. I think the controversy over this has been manufactured by the enemy to draw our attention away from the priority we should be giving to the Word of God.

My experience is to open up the Word of God, get on my knees before the open Bible, and begin reading not in a race to finish but in an attitude to receive. As I give God's Word priority in my life, He begins to honor that priority by unfolding to me what the Word of God is all about.

We will never understand the Bible through technology. Some try to prove the Bible to be false through technology and scientific experiments. You can prove anything you want to prove by using technology and science. The Bible does not yield itself to that sort of thing.

If I am going to know that the Bible is the Word of God, it will only come from the work of the Holy Spirit in my life. The Holy Spirit opens up the Word, reveals to me and illuminates to me the Lord Jesus Christ, who is the Living Word.

It would be impossible to say too much about the Bible. However, as a young Christian I became hungry for the Word of God. I wanted to read it and to meditate upon it. I did not have to memorize it, because as I meditated upon it, I began to learn it. Some people can memorize a verse of Scripture and not really know what it is talking about. I was storing it in my heart for the Spirit's ready access. The techniques of our study pale in comparison to the work of the Holy Spirit through the Word of God in our hearts.

My Daily Walk

The thing I want to stress as I close here is the word *daily*. My walk with God is a daily walk in cooperation with the Holy Spirit. The more I get to know the Holy Spirit, the more I will begin to understand the Bible and the gifts of the Spirit and the fruit of the Spirit and how God is doing things.

We try to explain the work of God from man's point of view. It is time—and this is the passion of my ministry—to begin explaining the work of God from God's perspective. As I get to know God, I begin to understand His perspective. Believe me, God's perspective is not the same as man's. God is working from the perspective of eternity, while man is working from the perspective of time.

My only hope for this book is that hearts will be stirred to seek God in the Word through the work of the Holy Spirit. No one is going to believe everything I say in this book. I challenge you to search the Scriptures and come to your own conclusions about what the Bible has to say about the Holy Spirit and the work of the Holy Spirit. Do not let me or anybody else form your opinion. Get on your knees with an open Bible, surrender yourself to the Holy Spirit, and see what He does in your life on a daily basis.

Nothing is greater than living a life in the Spirit.

Blessed Holy Spirit, I pray for the reader of this book, that You would deeply pierce his or her heart to the point of deep conviction. Out of that conviction, I pray will come a life that is truly alive in You. Amen.

A.W. Tozer (1897–1963) began his lifelong pursuit of God at the age of seventeen, after hearing a street preacher in Akron, Ohio. A self-taught theologian, Tozer was also a pastor, writer, and editor whose powerful use of words continues to grip the intellect and soul of today's believer. He authored more than forty books. *The Pursuit of God* and *The Knowledge of the Holy* are considered modern devotional classics.

Reverend James L. Snyder is an award-winning author whose writings have appeared in more than eighty periodicals and twenty-four books. He writes a weekly column, "Out to Pastor," that appears in nearly 300 newspapers across the country, both print and online. He is recognized as an authority on the life and ministry of A.W. Tozer, and received an honorary Doctor of Letters degree from Trinity College (Florida). His first book, *The Life of A.W. Tozer: In Pursuit of God*, won the Reader's Choice Award, in 1992, from *Christianity Today*. Because of his thorough knowledge of Tozer, James was given the rights from the A.W. Tozer estate to produce new books derived from over four hundred never-before-published audiotapes. James and his wife live in Ocala, Florida.

More from A.W. Tozer

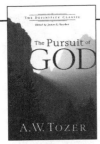

This enduring Christian classic is both thought-provoking and spirit-enlivening. A.W. Tozer invites you to think deeply about your faith and come alive to God's awe-inspiring presence that surrounds, sustains, and pursues you.

The Pursuit of God

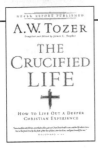

The apostle Paul declared, "I have been crucified with Christ." What exactly does this mean? This never-before published collection of Tozer's best teaching on the subject will give you a thorough understanding of the cross's centrality to your faith. At the heart of this book, you will find a call to follow Christ to the cross and be raised to new life—a call to live the crucified life.

The Crucified Life

Never-before-published, this is the message A.W. Tozer intended to be the follow-up to his seminal work *The Knowledge of the Holy*. Drawn from his sermons and papers, Tozer's teaching demonstrates how the attributes of God are a way to understand the essence of the Christian life—worship and service. Because we were created in the image of God, to understand who we are, we need to understand who God is and allow His character and nature to be reflected through us.

Delighting in God

More from A.W. Tozer

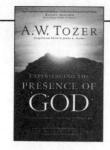

Deep in the soul of every person is a longing for the presence of God. But what does it mean to dwell in God's presence—and how do you get there? This collection of Tozer's teachings on the book of Hebrews shows you the way! As you explore this epistle's sweeping grasp of history and see your own struggles reflected in the "hero stories," you'll be led to experience the divine fulfillment for which you were created. Start dwelling in the presence of God today!

Experiencing the Presence of God

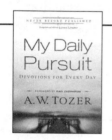

Let A.W. Tozer guide you in your pursuit of God with this 365-day devotional, full of never-before-published insights from a renowned servant of God. This book will challenge and inspire your heart and mind to truer worship, greater faith, deeper prayer, and more passion for Christ.

My Daily Pursuit

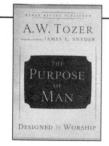

The Purpose of Man is the perfect introduction to Tozer. Drawn from messages he called his best teaching, this book will also delight those already familiar with, moved by, and changed by his other classics. What Tozer offers on the subject of worship here in *The Purpose of Man* will challenge you to reconsider your life's priorities while at the same time hold out a cup of Living Water for your soul.

The Purpose of Man